LETTERS TO FRIEND AND FOE

BARUCH SPINOZA

LETTERS TO
FRIEND AND FOE

Edited and with a Preface by
Dagobert D. Runes

Philosophical Library
New York

This collection is based, with minor changes and revisions, upon the translation from the Latin by R. H. M. Elwes.

Printed in the United States of America.

Distributed to the Trade by
BOOK SALES, INC.
352 Park Avenue South
New York, N.Y. 10010

PREFACE

The letters that appear in this volume cover only the last two decades of Spinoza's life and represent a mere fraction of the immense correspondence he carried on during his lifetime.

The story of Spinoza's expulsion from the synagogue of the small Jewish community in seventeenth-century Amsterdam is well known by now. Christianized Holland held the slight, dark-complexioned, sickly Jewish philosopher in equal disdain. Only the presence of such important friends as the Dutch statesman Jan de Witt and the powerful merchant Simon de Vries saved the outspoken Spinoza from prosecution by the Dutch authorities. As it was, during his lifetime and for a hundred years thereafter, practically all of Europe considered Spinoza a "dangerous" atheist. It was not until the latter part of the eighteenth century that the new era of enlightenment delivered Spinoza to his rightful place among the truly great philosophers of the world.

Indeed, the first edition of Spinoza's correspondence, which appeared in the year of his death, 1677, carried the notation: "Letters of some learned men to B.d.S. and the author's replies, which should contribute no little to the understanding of his other works." We see that even after his death it was still necessary to omit his name so that the distribution of his works might not be hampered.

One can readily understand, then, why so little of Spinoza's correspondence was saved for posterity. To retain an epistle signed by Spinoza was tantamount to foolhardiness because, although the Protestant Church of Holland had liberated itself from the rigidity and the brutal inquisition tactics practiced by the Spanish Catholics, it still used the most severe measures to deal with dissidents and heretics.

Spinoza spent the first half of his life in the intimacy of Amsterdam's Jewish community. His name appeared as late as 1655 among the donors for the celebration of Jewish religious holidays.

He was one of the most diligent students of the rabbinical school in the city and became steeped in the teachings and literature of Judaism. He had obtained much knowledge and developed a profound grasp of rabbinics. Nevertheless, his restless spirit did not permit him to serve as a cleric.

Among the people of Jewish Amsterdam there were great numbers of Marranos—Jews from Spain and Portugal who had managed to remain alive by the pretense of accepting Christianity. Arriving in Amsterdam, they desired to return to the faith of their fathers under the protection of the Dutch government. It is in this light that we must understand the anxiety of the local Jewish community concerning the religious well-being of these prodigal Jews, especially those of the young generation, whose adherence to Judaism was of very recent origin.

Judaism has always permitted dissidents and heretics to carry on what it considered a meaningless preoccupation. But here was a most unusual and difficult situation—one that called for action. The remnants of Spanish and Portuguese Jewry had been compelled to raise their children—at least officially—in a different faith. The Elders and the family fathers were desperate to bring their offspring back to the Covenant.

Then there came that rebellious youth, Spinoza, preaching a gospel of reform: Religion Without Ritualism; Faith Without Providence; A Universe Without a Personal God.

The Rabbis and the Elders pleaded with the adamant twenty-four-year-old student, whose father had died a little more than a year earlier, to desist. But he refused. The resultant expulsion from the synagogue was unavoidable. To Spinoza, it was a meaningless gesture (he offered, humorously, to explain to the Elders how to proceed with it). But it accomplished one thing: it cut Spinoza completely off from his Jewish friends and acquaintances in Amsterdam. He had to move to Ouderkerk, a suburb of the city, but within four years of his expulsion he went on to two little towns near The Hague and, finally, to The Hague itself.

During the years that he resided in the suburb of Amsterdam, he made his living as a teacher of the philosophy of Descartes— and as a teacher of Hebrew. In fact, he prepared textbooks on each of these subjects, Cartesianism as well as Hebrew grammar. In the year of his expulsion he wrote an Apologia in his mother tongue, Spanish, a pamphlet which has unfortunately been lost to history. While traces of this Apologia may be found in his *Theological-Political Tractate,* this book is somewhat marred by a chagrin against his people, who he felt had been unkind to him.

While such sentiment is understandable, one must also appreciate that the Jewish community of Amsterdam consisted of harassed refugees whose small number comprised one of the few remaining settlements in Western Europe that had escaped relentless Christian assault and persecution. At the time of Spinoza's expulsion from the synagogue, no Jew was permitted to live in England, Spain or Portugal. In other countries of Western Europe, such as Germany, France and what is today Italy, only a scattering of Jews survived—these in ghettos or by special local acts of "tolerance." In the east, especially in Poland during those very decades, 100,000 Jews were massacred in the most brutal manner by Russian Cossacks.

In such an era of tribulation the Jews had no time or patience with philosophical subtleties that might tend to undermine the cruelly tested faith of Jewish youth. The Jews expelled Spinoza not because they wanted to but, rather, because they had to. And yet, much of what appeared rebellious and heretical in that century is acceptable theology today—the then radical religious principles of Baruch Spinoza, for example, can today be considered cornerstones of Reform Judaism.

*   *   *

Most of the personal references and some of the letters containing such were omitted by the editors of the very first Latin edition of Spinoza's correspondence in order to avoid "differences" with the Protestant Church of Holland. Yet, through the pages of these theoretical and academic writings one can detect the brightness and be made aware of the dignity of Spinoza's thinking.

I felt it would be presumptuous on my part—nor did I think this little book the place—to burden it with annotations, explanations and interpretations concerning the recipients of the letters and their background.

I do hope these pages will inspire the readers to seek out the major works of the philosopher, the *Ethics* and the *Theological-Political Tractate.*

SPINOZA'S CORRESPONDENTS

Henry Oldenburg, German teacher and theologian
Georg Hermann Schuller, German physician
Simon de Vries, close friend and sponsor of Spinoza
Lewis Meyer, a physician, intimate of Spinoza
Peter Balling, Dutch merchant
Ehrenfried Walter von Tschirnhaus, German counselor
William de Blyenberg, Dutch merchant
Christian Huygens, eminent Dutch scientist
Albert Burgh, a young convert to Catholicism
Johannes Bouwmeester, (Bresser) physician
Jarig Jelles, Dutch merchant
Jacob Osten (Issac Orobio), surgeon in Utrecht
Lambert van Velthuysen, physician in Utrecht
Gottfried Wilhelm Leibniz, eminent German philosopher
J. Lewis Fabritius, professor at Heidelberg University
Hugo Boxel, Dutch city employee

SPINOZA'S

LETTERS TO FRIEND AND FOE

CONTENTS

CONTENTS

Spinoza to:

Baruch Spinoza

[Spinoza defines "God," and "attribute," and sends definitions, axioms, and first four propositions of Book I. of Ethics. Some errors of Bacon and Descartes discussed.]

ILLUSTRIOUS SIR, — How pleasant your friendship is to me, you may yourself judge, if your modesty will allow you to reflect on the abundance of your own excellences. Indeed the thought of these makes me seem not a little bold in entering into such a compact, the more so when I consider that between friends all things, and especially things spiritual, ought to be in common. However, this must lie at the charge of your modesty and kindness rather than of myself. You have been willing to lower yourself through the former and to fill me with the abundance of the latter, till I am no longer afraid to accept the close friendship, which you hold out to me, and which you deign to ask of me in return; no effort on my part shall be spared to render it lasting.

As for my mental endowments, such as they are, I would willingly allow you to share them, even though I knew it would be to my own great hindrance. But this is not meant as an excuse for denying to you what you ask by the rights of friendship. I will therefore endeavor to explain my opinions on the topics you touched on; though I scarcely hope, unless your kindness intervene, that I shall thus draw the bonds of our friendship closer.

I will then begin by speaking briefly of God, whom I define as a Being consisting in infinite attributes, whereof each is infinite or supremely perfect, after its kind. You must observe that by attribute I mean everything, which is conceived through itself and in itself, so that the conception of it does not involve the conception

13

of anything else. For instance, extension is conceived through itself and in itself, but motion is not. The latter is conceived through something else, for the conception of it implies extension.

That the definition above given of God is true appears from the fact, that by God we mean a Being supremely perfect and absolutely infinite. That such a Being exists may easily be proved from the definition; but as this is not the place for such proof, I will pass it over. What I am bound here to prove, in order to satisfy the first inquiry of my distinguished questioner, are the following consequences: FIRST, that in the universe there cannot exist two substances without their differing utterly in essence; SECONDLY, that substance cannot be produced or created—existence pertains to its actual essence; THIRDLY, that all substance must be infinite or supremely perfect after its kind.

When these points have been demonstrated, my distinguished questioner will readily perceive my drift, if he reflects at the same time on the definition of God. In order to prove them clearly and briefly, I can think of nothing better than to submit them to the bar of your judgment proved in the geometrical method.* I therefore enclose them separately and await your verdict upon them.

Again, you ask me what errors I detect in the Cartesian and Baconian philosophies. It is not my custom to expose the errors of others, nevertheless I will yield to your request. The first and the greatest error is, that these philosophers have strayed so far from the knowledge of the first cause and origin of all things; the second is, that they did not know the true nature of the human mind; the third, that they never grasped the true cause of error. The necessity for correct knowledge on these three points can only be ignored by persons completely devoid of learning and training.

That they have wandered astray from the knowledge of the first cause, and of the human mind, may easily be gathered from the truth of the three propositions given above; I therefore devote myself entirely to the demonstration of the third error. Of Bacon I shall say very

* The allusion is to Eth. I., Beginning—Prop. iv.

little, for he speaks very confusedly on the point, and works out scarcely any proofs: he simply narrates. In the first place he assumes that the human intellect is liable to err, not only through the fallibility of the senses, but also solely through its own nature, and that it frames its conceptions in accordance with the analogy of its own nature, not with the analogy of the universe, so that it is like a mirror receiving rays from external objects unequally, and mingling its own nature with the nature of things, etc.

Secondly, that the human intellect is, by reason of its own nature, prone to abstractions; such things as are in flux it feigns to be constant, etc.

Thirdly, that the human intellect continually augments, and is unable to come to a stand or to rest content. The other causes which he assigns may all be reduced to the one Cartesian principle, that the human will is free and more extensive than the intellect, or, as Verulam himself more confusedly puts it, that "the understanding is not a dry light, but receives infusion from the will." (We may here observe that Verulam often employs "intellect" as synonymous with mind, differing in this respect from Descartes.) This cause, then, leaving aside the others as unimportant, I shall show to be false; indeed its falsity would be evident to its supporters, if they would consider, that will in general differs from this or that particular volition in the same way as whiteness differs from this or that white object, or humanity from this or that man. It is, therefore, as impossible to conceive, that will is the cause of a given volition, as to conceive that humanity is the cause of Peter and Paul.

Hence, as will is merely an entity of the reason, and cannot be called the cause of particular volitions, and as some cause is needed for the existence of such volitions, these latter cannot be called free, but are necessarily such as they are determined by their causes; lastly, according to Descartes, errors are themselves particular volitions; hence it necessarily follows that errors, or, in other words, particular volitions, are not free, but are determined by external causes, and in nowise by the will. This is what I undertook to prove.

SPINOZA TO OLDENBURG.

[Spinoza answers some of Oldenburg's questions and doubts, but has not time to reply to all, as he is just setting out for Amsterdam.]

ILLUSTRIOUS SIR:— As I was starting for Amsterdam, where I intend staying for a week or two, I received your most welcome letter, and noted the objections you raise to the three propositions I sent you. Not having time to reply fully, I will confine myself to these three.

To the first I answer, that not from every definition does the existence of the thing defined follow, but only (as I showed in a note appended to the three propositions) from the definition or idea of an attribute, that is (as I explained fully in the definition given of God) of a thing conceived through and in itself. The reason for this distinction was pointed out, if I mistake not, in the above-mentioned note sufficiently clear at any rate for a philosopher, who is assumed to be aware of the difference between a fiction and a clear and distinct idea, and also of the truth of the axiom that every definition or clear and distinct idea is true. When this has been duly noted, I do not see what more is required for the solution of your first question.

I therefore proceed to the solution of the second, wherein you seem to admit that, if thought does not belong to the nature of extension, then extension will not be limited by thought; your doubt only involves the example given. But observe, I beg, if we say that extension is not limited by extension but by thought, is not this the same as saying that extension is not infinite absolutely, but only as far as extension is concerned, in other words, infinite after its kind? But you say: perhaps thought is a corporeal action: be it so, though I by no means grant it: you, at any rate, will not deny that extension, in so far as it is extension, is not thought, and this is all that is required for explaining my definition and proving the third proposition.

Thirdly. You proceed to object, that my axioms ought not to be ranked as universal notions. I will not dispute this point with you; but you further hesitate as to their truth, seeming to desire to show that their contrary is more probable. Consider, I beg, the definition which I gave of substance and attribute, for on that they all depend. When I say that I mean by substance that which is conceived through and in itself; and that I mean by modification or accident that, which is in something else, and is conceived through that wherein it is, evidently it follows that substance is by nature prior to its accidents. For without the former the latter can neither be nor be conceived. Secondly, it follows that, besides substances and accidents, nothing exists really or externally to the intellect. For everything is conceived either through itself or through something else, and the conception of it either involves or does not involve the conception of something else. Thirdly, it follows that things which possess different attributes have nothing in common. For by attribute I have explained that I mean something, of which the conception does not involve the conception of anything else. Fourthly, and lastly, it follows that, if two things have nothing in common, one cannot be the cause of the other. For, as there would be nothing in common between the effect and the cause, the whole effect would spring from nothing. As for your contention that God has nothing actually in common with created things, I have maintained the exact opposite in my definition. I said that God is a being consisting of infinite attributes, whereof each one is infinite or supremely perfect after its kind. With regard to what you say concerning my first proposition, I beg you, my friend, to bear in mind, that men are not created, but born, and that their bodies already exist before birth, though under different forms. You draw the conclusion, wherein I fully concur, that, if one particle of matter be annihilated, the whole of extension would forthwith vanish. My second proposition does not make many gods but only one, to wit, a Being consisting of infinite attributes, etc.

Spinoza to Oldenburg.

[Spinoza informs Oldenburg that he has removed to Rhijnsburg, and has spent some time at Amsterdam for the purpose of publishing the «Principles of Cartesian Philosophy.» He then replies to Boyle's objections.]

DISTINGUISHED SIR,— I have at length received your long wished for letter, and am at liberty to answer it. But, before I do so, I will briefly tell you, what has prevented my replying before. When I removed my household goods here in April, I set out for Amsterdam. While there certain friends asked me to impart to them a treatise containing, in brief, the second part of the principles of Descartes treated geometrically, together with some of the chief points treated of in metaphysics, which I had formerly dictated to a youth, to whom I did not wish to teach my own opinions openly. They further requested me, at the first opportunity, to compose a similar treatise on the first part. Wishing to oblige my friends, I at once set myself to the task, which I finished in a fortnight, and handed over to them. They then asked for leave to print it, which I readily granted on the condition that one of them should, under my supervision, clothe it in more elegant phraseology, and add a little preface warning readers that I do not acknowledge all the opinions there set forth as my own, inasmuch as I hold the exact contrary to much that is there written, illustrating the fact by one or two examples. All this the friend who took charge of the treatise promised to do, and this is the cause for my prolonged stay in Amsterdam. Since I returned to this village, I have hardly been able to call my time my own, because of the friends who have been kind enough to visit me. At last, my dear friend, a moment has come, when I can relate these occurrences to you, and inform you why I allow this treatise to see the light. It may be that on this occasion some of those, who hold the foremost positions in my country, will be found desirous of seeing the rest of my writings, which I acknowledge as my own; they will thus take care that I am enabled to publish them without any danger of infringing the laws of the land. If this be as I think, I shall doubtless publish at once; if things fall out otherwise, I would rather be silent than obtrude my opinions on men, in defiance of my country, and thus render them hostile to me. I therefore hope, my friend, that you will not chafe at having to wait a short time longer; you shall then receive from me either the treatise printed, or the summary of it which you ask for. If meanwhile you would like to have one or two copies of the work now in the press, I will satisfy your wish, as soon as I know of it and of means to send the book conveniently.

[The rest of the letter is taken up with criticisms on Boyle's book.]

SPINOZA TO OLDENBURG.

[Spinoza writes to his friend concerning the reasons which lead us to believe, that "every part of nature agrees with the whole, and is associated with all other parts." He also makes a few remarks about Huyghens.]

DISTINGUISHED SIR,— For the encouragement to pursue my speculations given me by yourself and the distinguished R. Boyle, I return you my best thanks. I proceed as far as my slender abilities will allow me, with full confidence in your aid and kindness. When you ask me my opinion on the question raised concerning our knowledge of the means, whereby each part of nature agrees with its whole, and the manner in which it is associated with the remaining parts, I presume you are asking for the reasons which induce us to believe, that each part of nature agrees with its whole, and is associated with the remaining parts. For as to the means whereby the parts are really associated, and each part agrees with its whole, I told you in my former letter that I am in ignorance. To answer such a question, we should have to know the whole of nature and its several parts. I will therefore endeavor to show the reason, which led me to make the statement; but I will premise that I do not attribute to nature either beauty or deformity, order or confusion. Only in relation to our imagination can things be called beautiful or deformed, ordered or confused.

By the association of parts, then, I merely mean that the laws or nature of one part adapt themselves to the laws or nature of another part, so as to cause the least possible inconsistency. As to the whole and the parts, I mean that a given number of things are parts of a whole, in so far as the nature of each of them is adapted to the nature of the rest, so that they all, as far as possible, agree together. On the other hand, in so far as they do not agree, each of them forms, in our mind, a separate idea, and is to that extent considered as a whole, not as a part. For instance, when the parts of lymph, chyle, etc., combine, according to the proportion of the figure and size of each, so as to evidently unite, and form one fluid, the chyle, lymph, etc., considered under this aspect, are part of the blood; but, in so far as we consider the particles of lymph as differing in figure and size from the particles of chyle, we shall consider each of the two as a whole, not as a part.

Let us imagine, with your permission, a little worm, living in the blood, able to distinguish by sight the particles of blood, lymph, etc., and to reflect on the manner in which each particle, on meeting with another particle, either is repulsed or communicates a portion of its own motion. This little worm would live in the blood, in the same way as we live in a part of the universe, and would consider each particle of blood, not as a part, but as a whole. He would be unable to determine how all the parts are modified by the general nature of blood, and are compelled by it to adapt themselves, so as to stand in a fixed relation to one another. For, if we imagine that there are no causes external to the blood, which could communicate fresh movements to it, nor any space beyond the blood, nor any bodies whereto the particles of blood could communicate their motion, it is certain that the blood would always remain in the same state, and its particles would undergo no modifications, save those which may be conceived as arising from the relations of motion existing between the lymph, the chyle, etc. The blood would then always have to be considered as a whole, not as a part. But, as there exist, as a matter of fact, very many causes which modify, in a given manner, the nature of the blood, and are, in turn, modified thereby, it follows that other motions and other relations arise in the blood, springing not from the mutual relations of its parts only, but from the mutual relations between the blood as a whole and external causes. Thus the blood comes to be regarded as a part, not as a whole. So much for the whole and the part.

All natural bodies can and ought to be considered in the same way as we have here considered the blood, for all bodies are surrounded by others, and are mutually determined to exist and operate in a fixed and definite proportion, while the relations between motion and rest in the sum total of them, that is, in the whole universe, remain unchanged. Hence it follows that each body, in so far as it exists as modified in a particular manner, must be considered as a part of the whole universe, as agreeing with the whole, and associated with the remaining parts. As the nature of the universe is not limited, like the nature of blood, but is absolutely infinite, its parts are by this nature of infinite power infinitely modified, and compelled to undergo infinite variations. But, in respect to substance, I conceive that each part has a more close union with its whole. For, as I said in my first letter (addressed to you while I was still at Rhijnsburg), substance being infinite in its nature,† it follows, as I endeavored to show. that each part belongs to the nature of substance, and without it, can neither be nor be conceived.

You see, therefore, how and why I think that the human body is a part of nature. As regards the human mind, I believe that it also is a part of nature; for I maintain that there exists in nature an infinite power of thinking, which, in so far as it is infinite, contains subjectively the whole of nature, and its thoughts proceed in the same manner as nature — that is, in the sphere of ideas. Further, I take the human mind to be identical with this said power, not in so far as it is infinite and perceives the whole nature, but in so far as it is finite, and perceives only the human body; in this manner, I maintain that the human mind is a part of an infinite understanding.

But to explain, and accurately prove, all these and kindred questions, would take too long; and I do not think you expect as much of me at present. I am afraid that I may have mistaken your meaning, and given an answer to a different question from that which you asked. Please inform me on this point.

You write in your last letter, that I hinted that nearly all the Cartesian laws of motion are false. What I said was, if I remember rightly, that Huyghens think so ; I myself do not impeach any of the laws except the sixth, concerning which I think Huyghens is also in error. I ask you at the same time to communicate to me the experiment made according to that hypothesis in your Royal Society; as you have not replied, I infer that you are not at liberty to do so. The above-mentioned Huyghens is entirely occupied in polishing lenses. He has fitted up for the purpose a handsome workshop, in which he can also construct molds. What will be the result I know not, nor, to speak the truth, do I greatly care. Experience has sufficiently taught me, that the free hand is better and more sure than any machine for polishing spherical molds. I can tell you nothing certain as yet about the success of the clocks or the date of Huyghens's journey to France.

SPINOZA TO OLDENBURG.

[Spinoza relates his journey to Amsterdam for the purpose of publishing his « Ethics »; he was deterred by the dissuasions of theologians and Cartesians. He hopes that Oldenburg will inform him of some of the objections to the « Tractatus Theologico-Politicus, » made by learned men, so that they may be answered in notes.]

Distinguished and Illustrious Sir,—When I received your letter of the 22nd July, I had set out to Amsterdam for the purpose of publishing the book I had mentioned to you. While I was negotiating, a rumor gained currency that I had in the press a book concerning God, wherein I endeavored to show that there is no God. This report was believed by many. Hence certain theologians, perhaps the authors of the rumor, took occasion to complain of me before the prince and the magistrates; moreover, the stupid Cartesians, being suspected of favoring me, endeavored to remove the aspersion by abusing everywhere my opinions and writings, a course which they still pursue. When I became aware of this through trustworthy men, who also assured me that the theologians were everywhere lying in wait for me, I determined to put off publishing till I saw how things were going, and I proposed to inform you of my intentions. But matters seem to get worse and worse, and I am still uncertain what to do. Meanwhile I do not like to delay any longer answering your letter. I will first thank you heartily for your friendly warning, which I should be glad to have further explained, so that I may know, which are the doctrines which seem to you to be aimed against the practice of religion and virtue. If principles agree with reason, they are, I take it, also most serviceable to virtue. Further, if it be not troubling you too much I beg you to point out the passages in the "Tractatus Theologico-Politicus" which are objected to by the learned, for I want to illustrate that treatise with notes, and to remove if possible the prejudices conceived against it. Farewell.

Spinoza to Oldenburg.

Distinguished Sir,— I received on Saturday last your very short letter dated 15th Nov. In it you merely indicate the points in the theological treatise, which have given pain to readers, whereas I had hoped to learn from it, what were the opinions which militated against the practice of religious virtue, and which you formerly mentioned. However, I will speak on the three subjects on which you desire me to disclose my sentiments, and tell you, first, that my opinion concerning God differs widely from that which is ordinarily defended by modern Christians. For I hold that God is of all things the cause immanent, as the phrase is, not transient. I say that all things are in God and move in God, thus agreeing with Paul, and, perhaps, with all the ancient philosophers, though the phraseology may be different; I will even venture to affirm that I agree with all the ancient Hebrews, in so far as one may judge from their traditions, though these are in many ways corrupted. The supposition of some, that I endeavor to prove in the "Tractatus Theologico-Politicus" the unity of God and Nature (meaning by the latter a certain mass or corporeal matter), is wholly erroneous.

As regards miracles, I am of opinion that the revelation of God can only be established by the wisdom of the doctrine, not by miracles, or in other words, by ignorance. This I have shown at sufficient length in Chapter VI. concerning miracles. I will here only add, that I make this chief distinction between religion and superstition, that the latter is founded on ignorance, the former on knowledge; this, I take it, is the reason why Christians are distinguished from the rest of the world, not by faith, nor by charity, nor by the other fruits of the Holy Spirit, but solely by their opinions, inasmuch as they defend their cause, like everyone else, by miracles, that is, by ignorance, which is the source of all malice; thus they turn a faith, which may be true, into superstition. Lastly, in order to disclose my opinions on the third point, I will tell you that I do not think it necessary for salvation to know Christ according to the flesh: but with regard to the Eternal Son of God, that is, the Eternal Wisdom of God, which has manifested itself in all things and especially in the human mind, and above all in Christ Jesus, the case is far otherwise. For without this no one can come to a state of blessedness, inasmuch as it alone teaches, what is true or false, good

24

or evil. And, inasmuch as this wisdom was made especially manifest through Jesus Christ, as I have said, his disciples preached it, in so far as it was revealed to them through him, and thus showed that they could rejoice in that spirit of Christ more than the rest of mankind. The doctrines added by certain churches, such as that God took upon himself human nature, I have expressly said that I do not understand; in fact, to speak the truth, they seem to me no less absurd than would a statement, that a circle had taken upon itself the nature of a square. This I think will be sufficient explanation of my opinions concerning the three points mentioned. Whether it will be satisfactory to Christians you will know better than I. Farewell.

SPINOZA TO OLDENBURG.

[Spinoza expounds to Oldenburg his views on fate and necessity, discriminates between miracles and ignorance, takes the resurrection of Christ as spiritual, and deprecates attributing to the sacred writers western modes of speech.]

DISTINGUISHED SIR:— At last I see what it was that you begged me not to publish. However, as it forms the chief foundation of everything in the treatise which I intended to bring out, I should like briefly to explain here in what sense I assert that a fatal necessity presides over all things and actions. God I in no wise subject to fate: I conceive that all things follow with inevitable necessity from the nature of God, in the same way as every one conceives that it follows from God's nature that God understands himself. This latter consequence all admit to follow necessarily from the divine nature, yet no one conceives that God is under the compulsion of any fate, but that he understands himself quite freely, though necessarily.

Further, this inevitable necessity in things does away neither with divine nor human laws. The principles of morality, whether they receive from God himself the form of laws or institutions, or whether they do not, are still divine and salutary; whether we receive the good, which flows from virtue and the divine love, as from God in the capacity of a judge, or as from the necessity of the divine nature, it will in either case be equally desirable; on the other hand, the evils following from wicked actions and passions are not less to be feared because they are necessary consequences. Lastly, in our actions, whether they be necessary or contingent, we are led by hope and fear.

Men are only without excuse before God, because they are in God's power, as clay is in the hands of the potter, who from the same lump makes vessels, some to honor, some to dishonor. If you will reflect a little on this, you will, I doubt not, easily be able to reply to any objections which may be urged against my opinion, as many of my friends have already done.

I have taken miracles and ignorance as equivalent terms, because those, who endeavor to establish God's existence and the truth of religion by means of miracles, seek to prove the obscure by what is more obscure and completely unknown, thus introducing a new sort of argument, the reduction, not to the impossible, as the phrase is, but to ignorance. But, if I mistake not, I have sufficiently explained my opinion on miracles in the »Theologico-Political» treatise. I will only add here, that if you will reflect on the facts; that Christ did not appear to the council, nor to Pilate, nor to any unbeliever, but only to the faithful; also that God has neither right hand nor left, but is by his essence not in a particular spot, but everywhere; that matter is everywhere the same; that God does not manifest himself in the imaginary space supposed to be outside the world; and lastly, that the frame of the human body is kept within due limits solely by the weight of the air; you will readily see that this apparition of Christ is not unlike that wherewith God appeared to Abraham, when the latter saw men whom he invited to dine with him. But, you will say, all the Apostles thoroughly believed, that Christ rose from the dead and really ascended to heaven: I do not deny it. Abraham, too, believed that God had dined with him, and all the Israelites believed that God descended, surrounded with fire, from heaven to Mount Sinai, and there spoke directly with them; whereas, these apparitions or revelations, and many others like them, were adapted to the understanding and opinions of those men, to whom God wished thereby to reveal his will. I therefore conclude, that the resurrection of Christ from the dead was in reality spiritual, and that to the faithful alone, according to their understanding, it was revealed that Christ was endowed with eternity, and had risen from the dead (using DEAD in the sense in which Christ said, "let the dead bury their dead" *), giving by his life and death a matchless example of holiness. Moreover, he to this extent raises his disciples from the dead, in so far as they follow the example of his own life and death. It would not be difficult to explain the whole Gospel doctrine on this hypothesis. Nay, 1 Cor. ch. xv. cannot be explained on any other, nor can Paul's arguments be understood: if we follow the common interpretation, they appear weak and can easily be refuted: not to mention the fact, that Christians interpret spiritually all those doctrines which the Jews accepted literally. I join with you in acknowledging human weakness. But on the other hand, I venture to ask you whether we " human pigmies " possess sufficient knowledge of nature to be able to lay down the limits of its force and power, or to say that a given thing surpasses that power? No one could go so far without arrogance. We may, therefore, without presumption explain miracles as far as possible by natural causes. When we cannot explain them, nor even prove their impossibility, we may well suspend our judgment about them, and establish religion, as I have said, solely by the wisdom of its doctrines. You think that the texts in John's Gospel and in Hebrews are inconsistent with what I advance, because you measure oriental phrases by the standards of European speech; though John wrote his gospel in Greek, he wrote it as a Hebrew. However this may be, do you believe, when Scripture says that God manifested himself in a cloud, or that he dwelt in the tabernacle, or the temple, that God actually assumed the nature of a cloud, a tabernacle, or a temple? Yet the ut-

* Matt. viii. 22; Luke ix. 60.

most that Christ says of himself, that he is the Temple of God,* because, as I said before, God had specially manifested himself in Christ. John, wishing to express the same truth more forcibly, said that "the Word was made flesh." But I have said enough on the subject.

Written 7 Feb., 1676.

SPINOZA TO OLDENBURG.

[Spinoza again treats of fatalism. He repeats that he accepts Christ's passion, death, and burial literally, but his resurrection spiritually.]

DISTINGUISHED SIR,—When I said in my former letter that we are inexcusable, because we are in the power of God, like clay in the hands of the potter, I meant to be understood in the sense that no one can bring a complaint against God for having given him a weak nature, or infirm spirit. A circle might as well complain to God of not being endowed with the properties of a sphere, or a child who is tortured, say, with stone, for not being given a healthy body, as a man of feeble spirit, because God has denied to him fortitude, and the true knowledge and love of the Deity, or because he is endowed with so weak a nature that he cannot check or moderate his desires. For the nature of each thing is only competent to do that which follows necessarily from its given cause. That every man cannot be brave, and that we can no more command for ourselves a healthy body than a healthy mind, nobody can deny, without giving the lie to experience, as well as to reason. "But," you urge, "if men sin by nature, they are excusable"; but you do not state the conclusion you draw, whether that God cannot be angry with them or that they are worthy of blessedness—that is, of the knowledge and love of God. If you say the former, I fully admit that God cannot be angry, and that all things are done in accordance with his will; but I deny that all men ought, therefore, to be blessed—men may be excusable, and, nevertheless, be without blessedness and afflicted in many ways. A horse is excusable for being a horse and not a man; but, never-theless, he must needs be a horse and not a man. He who goes mad from the bite of a dog is excusable, yet he is rightly suffocated. Lastly, he who cannot govern his desires, and keep them in check with the fear of the laws, though his weakness may be excusable, yet he can-not enjoy with contentment the knowledge and love of God, but necessarily perishes. I do not think it neces-sary here to remind you, that Scripture, when it says that God is angry with sinners, and that he is a Judge who takes cognizance of human actions, passes sentence on them, and judges them, is speaking humanely, and in a way adapted to the received opinion of the masses, inasmuch as its purpose is not to teach phi-losophy, nor to render men wise, but to make them obedient.

How, by taking miracles and ignorance as equiva-lent terms, I reduce God's power and man's knowl-edge within the same limits, I am unable to discern.

For the rest, I accept Christ's passion, death and burial literally, as you do, but his resurrection I understand allegorically. I admit, that it is related by the Evangelists in such detail, that we cannot deny that they themselves believed Christ's body to have risen from the dead and ascended to heaven, in order to sit at the right hand of God, or that they believed that Christ might have been seen by unbelievers, if they had happened to be at hand, in the places where he appeared to his Disciples; but in these matters they might, without injury to Gospel teach-ing, have been deceived, as was the case with other prophets mentioned in my last letter. But Paul, to whom Christ afterward appeared, rejoices that he knew Christ not after the flesh, but after the spirit.* Farewell, hon-orable Sir, and believe me yours in all affection and zeal

SPINOZA TO SIMON DE VRIES.

[Spinoza deprecates his correspondent's jealousy of Albert Burgh; and answers that distinction must be made between different kinds of definitions. He explains his opinions more precisely.]

* 2 Cor. v. 16

RESPECTED FRIEND,—I have received your long wished-for letter, for which, and for your affection toward me, I heartily thank you. Your long absence has been no less grievous to me than to you; yet in the meantime I rejoice that my trifling studies are of profit to you and our friends. For thus while you are away, I in my absence speak to you. You need not envy my fellow-lodger. There is no one who is more displeasing to me, nor against whom I have been more anxiously on my guard; and therefore I would have you and all my acquaintance warned not to communicate my opinions to him, except when he has come to maturer years. So far he is too childish and inconstant, and is fonder of novelty than of truth. But I hope, that in a few years he will amend these childish faults. Indeed I am almost sure of it, as far as I can judge from his nature. And so his temperament bids me like him.

As for the questions propounded in your club, which is wisely enough ordered, I see that your difficulties arise from not distinguishing between kinds of definition: that is, b̲e̲t̲ ̲.̲.̲.̲ ̲a̲ ̲definition serving to explain a thing, of which the essence only is sought and in question, and a definition which is put forward only for purposes of inquiry. The former having a definite object ought to be true, the latter need not. For instance, if some one asks me for a description of Solomon's temple, I am bound to give him a true description, unless I want to talk nonsense with him. But if I have constructed, in my mind, a temple which I desire to build, and infer from the description of it that I must buy such and such a site and so many thousand stones and other materials, will any sane person tell me that I have drawn a wrong conclusion because my definition is possibly untrue? or will anyone ask me to prove my definition? Such a person would simply be telling me, that I had not conceived that which I had conceived, or be requiring me to prove, that I had conceived that which I had conceived; in fact, evidently trifling. Hence a definition either explains a thing, in so far as it is external to the intellect, in which case it ought to be true and only to differ from a proposition or an axiom in being concerned merely with the essences of things, or the modifications of things, whereas the latter has a wider scope and extends also to eternal truths. Or else it explains a thing, as it is conceived or can be conceived by us; and then it differs from an axiom or proposition, inasmuch as it only requires to be conceived absolutely, and not like an axiom as true. Hence a bad definition is one which is not conceived. To explain my meaning, I will take Borel's example — a man saying that two straight lines enclosing a space shall be called " figurals." If the man means by a straight line the same as the rest of the world means by a curved line, his definition is good (for by the definition would be meant some such figure as (), or the like); so long as he does not afterward mean a square or other kind of figure. But, if he attaches the ordinary meaning to the words straight line, the thing is evidently inconceivable, and therefore there is no definition. These considerations are plainly confused by Borel, to whose opinion you incline. I give another example, the one you cite at the end of your letter. If I say that each substance has only one attribute, this an unsupported statement and needs ᵣ ᵒᵒᶠ but, if I say that I mean by substance that which cons. 's in only one attribute, the definition will be good, so long as entities consisting of several attributes are afterward styled by some name other than substance. When you say that I do not prove, that substance (or being) may have several attributes, you do not perhaps pay attention to the proofs given. I adduced two: First, "that nothing is plainer to us, than that every being may be conceived by us under some attribute, and that the more reality or essence a given being has, the more attributes may be attributed to it. Hence a being absolutely infinite must be defined, etc." Secondly, and I think this is the stronger proof of the two, "the more attributes I assign to any being, the more am I compelled to assign to it existence;" in other words, the more I conceive it as true. The contrary would evidently result if I were feigning a chimera or some such being.

Your remark that you cannot conceive thought except

as consisting in ideas, because, when ideas are removed, thought is annihilated, springs, I think, from the fact that while you a thinking thing, do as you say, you abstract all your thoughts and conceptions. It is no marvel that, when you have abstracted all your thoughts and conceptions, you have nothing left for thinking with. On the general subject, I think I have shown sufficiently clearly and plainly, that the intellect, although infinite, belongs to nature regarded as passive rather than nature regarded as active (*ad naturam naturatam, non vero ad naturam naturantem*).

However, I do not see how this helps toward understanding the third definition, nor what difficulty the latter presents. It runs, if I mistake not, as follows: "By substance I mean that, which is in itself and is conceived through itself; that is, of which the conception does not involve the conception of anything else. By attribute I mean the same thing; except that it is called attribute with respect to the understanding, which attributes to substance the particular nature aforesaid." This definition, I repeat, explains with sufficient clearness what I wish to signify by substance or attribute. You desire, though there is no need, that I should illustrate by an example, how one and the same thing can be stamped with two names. In order not to seem miserly, I will give you two. First, I say that by Israel is meant the third patriarch; I mean the same by Jacob, the name Jacob being given, because the patriarch in question had caught hold of the heel of his brother. Secondly, by a colorless surface I mean a surface, which reflects all rays of light without altering them. I mean the same by a white surface, with this difference, that a surface is called white in reference to a man looking at it, etc.

SPINOZA TO SIMON DE VRIES.

[Spinoza, in answer to a letter from De Vries now lost, speaks of the experience necessary for proving a definition, and also of eternal truths.]

RESPECTED FRIEND,—You ask me if we have need of

experience, in order to know whether the definition of a given attribute is true. To this I answer that we never need experience, except in cases when the existence of the thing cannot be inferred from its definition, as, for instance, the existence of modes (which cannot be inferred from their definition); experience is not needed, when the existence of the things in question is not distinguished from their essence, and is therefore inferred from their definition. This can never be taught us by any experience, for experience does not teach us any essences of things; the utmost it can do is to set our mind thinking about definite essences only. Wherefore, when the existence of attributes does not differ from their essence, no experience is capable of attaining it for us.

To your further question, whether things and their modifications are eternal truths, I answer; Certainly. If you ask me, why I do not call them eternal truths, I answer, in order to distinguish them, in accordance with general usage, from those propositions, which do not make manifest any particular thing or modification of a thing; for example, NOTHING COMES FROM NOTHING. These and such like propositions are, I repeat, called eternal truths simply, the meaning merely being, that they have no standpoint external to the mind, etc.

SPINOZA TO LEWIS MEYER

DEAREST FRIEND,—I have received two letters from you, one dated Jan. 11, delivered to me by our friend, N. N., the other dated March 26, sent by some unknown friend to Leyden. They were both most welcome to me, especially as I gathered from them, that all goes well with you, and that you are often mindful of me. I also owe and repay you the warmest thanks for the courtesy and consideration, with which you have always been kind enough to treat me: I hope you will believe, that I am in no less degree devoted to you, as, when occasion offers, I will always endeavor to prove, as far as my poor powers will admit. As a first proof, I will do my best to answer the questions you ask in your letters. You request me to tell you, what I think about the Infinite; I will most readily do so.

Everyone regards the question of the Infinite as most difficult, if not insoluble, through not making a distinction between that which must be infinite from its very nature, or in virtue of its definition, and that which has no limits, not in virtue of its essence, but in virtue of its cause; and also through not distinguishing between that which is called infinite, because it has no limits, and that, of which the parts cannot be equalled or expressed by any number, though the greatest and least magnitude of the whole may be known; and, lastly, through not distinguishing between that, which can be understood but not imagined, and that which can also be imagined. If these distinctions, I repeat, had been attended to, inquirers would not have been overwhelmed with such a vast crowd of difficulties. They would then clearly have understood, what kind of infinite is indivisible and possesses no parts; and what kind, on the other hand, may be divided without involving a contradiction in terms. They would further have understood, what kind of infinite may, without solecism, be conceived greater than another infinite, and what kind cannot be so conceived. All this will plainly appear from what I am about to say.

However, I will first briefly explain the terms SUBSTANCE, MODE, ETERNITY, and DURATION.

The points to be noted concerning substance are these: First, that existence appertains to its essence; in other words, that solely from its essence and definition its existence follows. This, if I remember rightly, I have already proved to you by word of mouth, without the id of any other propositions. Secondly, as a consequence of the above, that substance is not manifold, but single: there cannot be two of the same nature. Thirdly, every substance must be conceived as infinite.

The modifications of substance I call MODES. Their definition, in so far as it is not identical with that of sub-

Spinoza's Workroom at Rijnsburg.

The instruments that Spinoza used for his work as a maker of lenses are on the table.

stance, cannot involve any existence. Hence, though they exist, we can conceive them as non-existent. From this it follows, that, when we are regarding only the essence of modes, and not the order of the whole of nature, we cannot conclude from their present existence, that they will exist or not exist in the future, or that they have existed or not existed in the past; whence it is abundantly clear, that we conceive the existence of substance as entirely different from the existence of modes. From this difference arises the distinction between ETERNITY and DURATION. DURATION is only applicable to the existence of modes; ETERNITY is applicable to the existence of substance, that is, the infinite faculty of existence or being (*infinitum existendi sive — invitâ Latinitate — essendi fruitionem*).

From what has been said it is quite clear that when, as is most often the case, we are regarding only the essence of modes and not the order of nature, we may freely limit the existence and duration of modes without destroying the conception we have formed of them; we may conceive them as greater or less, or may divide them into parts. Eternity and substance, being only conceivable as infinite, cannot be thus treated without our conception of them being destroyed. Wherefore it is mere foolishness, or even insanity, to say that extended substance is made up of parts or bodies really distinct from one another. It is as though one should attempt by the aggregation and addition of many circles to make up a square, or a triangle, or something of totally different essence. Wherefore the whole heap of arguments, by which philosophers commonly endeavor to show that extended substance is finite, falls to the ground by its own weight. For all such persons suppose, that corporeal substance is made up of parts. In the same way, others who have persuaded themselves that a line is made up of points, have been able to discover many arguments to show that a line is not infinitely divisible. If you ask, why we are by nature so prone to attempt to divide extended substance, I answer, that quantity is conceived by us in two ways, namely, by abstraction or superficially, as we

35

imagine it by the aid of the senses, or as substance, which can only be accomplished through the understanding. So that, if we regard quantity as it exists in the imagination (and this is the more frequent and easy method), it will be found to be divisible, finite, composed of parts, and manifold. But, if we regard it as it is in the understanding, and the thing be conceived as it is in itself (which is very difficult), it will then, as I have sufficiently shown you before, be found to be infinite, indivisible, and single.

Again, from the fact that we can limit duration and quantity at our pleasure, when we conceive the latter abstractedly as apart from substance, and separate the former from the manner whereby it flows from things eternal, there arise TIME and MEASURE; TIME for the purpose of limiting duration, MEASURE for the purpose of limiting quantity, so that we may, as far as is possible, the more readily imagine them. Further, inasmuch as we separate the modifications of substance from substance itself, and reduce them to classes, so that we may, as far as is possible, the more readily imagine them, there arises NUMBER, whereby we limit them. Whence it is clearly to be seen, that measure, time, and number, are merely modes of thinking, or, rather, of imagining. It is not to be wondered at, therefore, that all who have endeavored to understand the course of nature, by means of such notions, and without fully understanding even them, have entangled themselves so wondrously, that they have at last only been able to extricate themselves by breaking through every rule and admitting absurdities even of the grossest kind. For there are many things which cannot be conceived through the imagination but only through the understanding, for instance, substance, eternity, and the like; thus, if any one tries to explain such things by means of conceptions which are mere aids to the imagination, he is simply assisting his imagination to run away with him. Nor can even the modes of substance ever be rightly understood, if we confuse them with entities of the kind mentioned, mere aids of the reason or imagination. In so doing we separate them from substance, and the mode of their derivation from eternity, without which they can never be rightly understood. To make the matter yet more clear, take the following example: when a man conceives of duration abstractedly, and, confusing it with time, begins to divide it into parts, he will never be able to understand how an hour, for instance, can elapse. For in order that an hour should elapse, it is necessary that its half should elapse first, and afterward half of the remainder, and again half of the half of the remainder, and if you go on thus to infinity, subtracting the half of the residue, you will never be able to arrive at the end of the hour. Wherefore many, who are not accustomed to distinguish abstractions from realities, have ventured to assert that duration is made up of instants, and so in wishing to avoid Charybdis have fallen into Scylla. It is the same thing to make up duration out of instants, as it is to make number simply by adding up naughts.

Further, as it is evident from what has been said, that neither number, nor measure, nor time, being mere aids to the imagination, can be infinite (for, otherwise, number would not be number, nor measure measure, nor time time); it is hence abundantly evident, why many who confuse these three abstractions with realities, through being ignorant of the true nature of things, have actually denied the Infinite.

The wretchedness of their reasoning may be judged by mathematicians, who have never allowed themselves to be delayed a moment by arguments of this sort, in the case of things which they clearly and distinctly perceive. For not only have they come across many things, which cannot be expressed by number (thus showing the inadequacy of number for determining all things); but also they have found many things, which cannot be equalled by any number, but surpass every possible number. But they infer hence, that such things surpass enumeration, not because of the multitude of their component parts, but because their nature cannot, without manifest contradiction, be expressed in terms of number. As, for instance, in the case of two circles, non-concentric, whereof one incloses the other, no number can express the inequalities of distance which exist between the two circles, nor all the variations which matter in motion in the intervening space may undergo. This conclusion is not based on the excessive size of the intervening space. However small a portion of it we take, the inequalities of this small portion will surpass all numerical expression. Nor, again, is the conclusion based on the fact, as in other cases, that we do not know the maximum and the minimum of the said space. It springs simply from the fact, that the nature of the space between two non-concentric circles cannot be expressed in number. Therefore, he who would assign a numerical equivalent for the inequalities in question, would be bound, at the same time, to bring about that a circle should not be a circle.

The same result would take place — to return to my subject — if one were to wish to determine all the motions undergone by matter up to the present, by reducing them and their duration to a certain number and time. This would be the same as an attempt to deprive corporeal substance, which we cannot conceive except as existent, of its modifications, and to bring about that it should not possess the nature which it does possess. All this I could clearly demonstrate here, together with many other points touched on in this latter, but I deem it superfluous.

From all that has been said, it is abundantly evident that certain things are in their nature infinite, and can by no means be conceived as finite; whereas there are other things, infinite in virtue of the cause from which they are derived, which can, when conceived abstractedly, be divided into parts, and regarded as finite. Lastly, there are some which are called infinite or, if you prefer, indefinite, because they cannot be expressed in number, which may yet be conceived as greater or less. It does not follow that such are equal, because they are alike incapable of numerical expression. This is plain enough, from the example given, and many others.

Lastly, I have put briefly before you the causes of error and confusion, which have arisen concerning the question of the infinite. I have, if I mistake not, so explained them that no question concerning the infinite remains untreated, or cannot readily be solved from what I have said; wherefore, I do not think it worth while to detain you longer on the matter.

But I should like it first to be observed here, that the later Peripatetics have, I think, misunderstood the proof given by the Ancients who sought to demonstrate the existence of God. This, as I find it in a certain Jew named Rabbi Ghasdai, runs as follows: "If there be an infinite series of causes, all things which are, are caused. But nothing which is caused can exist necessarily in virtue of its own nature. Therefore, there is nothing in nature, to whose essence existence necessarily belongs. But this is absurd. Therefore, the premise is absurd also." Hence the force of the argument lies not in the impossibility of an actual infinite or an infinite series of causes; but only in the absurdity of the assumption that things, which do not necessarily exist by nature, are not conditioned for existence by a thing, which does by its own nature necessarily exist.

I would now pass on, for time presses, to your second letter: but I shall be able more conveniently to reply to its contents, when you are kind enough to pay me a visit. I therefore beg that you will come as soon as possible; the time for traveling is at hand. Enough. Farewell, and keep in remembrance,

Yours, etc.

RHIJNSBURG, 20 April, 1663.

SPINOZA TO LEWIS MEYER.

DEAR FRIEND,—The preface you sent me by our friend De Vries, I now send back to you by the same hand. Some few things, as you will see, I have marked in the margin; but yet a few remain, which I have judged it better to mention to you by letter. First, where on page 4 you give the reader to know on what occasion I composed the first part; I would have you likewise explain there, or where you please, that I composed it within a fortnight. For when this is explained none will suppose the exposition to be so clear as that it cannot be bettered, and so they will not stick at obscurities in this and that phrase on which they may chance to stumble. Secondly, I would have you explain, that when I prove many points otherwise than they be proved by Descartes, 'tis not to amend Descartes, but the better to preserve my order, and not to multiply axioms overmuch: and that for this same reason I prove many things which by Descartes are barely alleged without any proof, and must needs add other matters which Descartes let alone. Lastly, I will earnestly beseech you, as my especial friend, to let be everything you have written toward the end against that creature, and wholly strike it out. And though many reasons determine me to this request, I will give but one. I would fain have all men readily believe that these matters are published for the common profit of the world, and that your sole motive in bringing out the book is the love of spreading the truth; and that it is accordingly all your study to make the work acceptable to all, to bid men, with all courtesy to the pursuit of genuine philosophy, and to consult their common advantage. Which every man will be ready to think when he sees that no one is attacked, nor anything advanced where any man can find the least offense. Notwithstanding, if afterward the person you know of, or any other, be minded to display his ill-will, then you may portray his life and character, and gain applause by it. So I ask that you will not refuse to be patient thus far, and suffer yourself to be entreated, and believe me wholly bounden to you, and

Yours with all affection

B. DE SPINOZA.

VOORBURG, Aug. 3, 1663.

Our friend De Vries had promised to take this with him; but seeing he knows not when he will return to you, I send it by another hand.

Along with this I send you part of the scholium to Prop. xxvii. Part II. where page 75 begins, that you may hand it to the printer to be reprinted. The matter I send you must of necessity be reprinted, and fourteen or fifteen lines added, which may easily be inserted.

SPINOZA TO PETER BALLING.

[Concerning omens and phantoms. The mind may have a confused presentiment of the future.]

BELOVED FRIEND,— Your last letter, written, if I mistake not, on the 26th of last month, has duly reached me. It caused me no small sorrow and solicitude, though the feeling sensibly diminished when I reflected on the good sense and fortitude, with which you have known how to despise the evils of fortune, or rather of opinion, at a time when they most bitterly assailed you. Yet my anxiety increases daily; I therefore beg and implore you by the claims of our friendship, that you will rouse yourself to write me a long letter. With regard to OMENS, of which you make mention in telling me that, while your child was still healthy and strong, you heard groans like those he uttered when he was ill and shortly afterward died, I should judge that these were not real groans, but only the effect of your imagination; for you say that, when you got up and composed yourself to listen, you did not hear them so clearly either as before or as afterward, when you had fallen asleep again. This, I think, shows that the groans were purely due to the imagination, which, when it was unfettered and free, could imagine groans more forcibly and vividly than when you sat up in order to listen in a particular direction. I think I can both illustrate and confirm what I say by another occurrence, which befell me at Rhijnsburg last winter. When one morning, after the day had dawned, I woke up from a very unpleasant dream, the images, which had presented themselves to me in sleep, remained before my eyes just as vividly as though the things had been real, especially the image of a certain black and leprous Brazilian whom I had never seen before. This image disappeared for the most part when, in order to divert my thoughts, I cast my eyes on a book, or something else. But, as soon as I lifted my eyes again without fixing my attention on any particular object, the same image of this same negro appeared with the same vividness again and again, until the head of it gradually vanished. I say that the same thing which occurred with regard to my inward sense of sight, occurred with your hearing; but as the causes were very different, your case was an omen and mine was not. The matter may be clearly grasped by means of what I am about to say. The effects of the imagination arise either from bodily or mental causes. I will proceed to prove this, in order not to be too long, solely from experience. We know that fevers and other bodily ailments are the causes of delirium, and that persons of stubborn disposition imagine nothing but quarrels, brawls, slaughterings, and the like. We also see that the imagination is to a certain extent determined by the character of the disposition, for, as we know by experience, it follows in the tracks of the understanding in every respect, and arranges its images and words, just as the understanding arranges its demonstrations and connects one with another; so that we are hardly at all able to say what will not serve the imagination as a basis for some image or other. This being so, I say that no effects of imagination springing from physical causes can ever be omens of future events; inasmuch as their causes do not involve any future events. But the effects of imagination, or images originating in the mental disposition, may be omens of some future event; inasmuch as the mind may have a confused presentiment of the future. It may, therefore, imagine a future event as forcibly and vividly, as though it were present; for instance a father (to take an example resembling your own) loves his child so much that he and the beloved child are, as it were, one and the same. And since (like that which I demonstrated on another occasion) there must necessarily exist in thought the idea of the essence of the child's states and their results, and since the father, through his union with his child, is a part of the said child, the soul of the father must necessarily participate in the ideal essence of the child and his states, and in their results, as I have shown at greater length elsewhere.

Again, as the soul of the father participates ideally in the consequences of his child's essence, he may (as I have said) sometimes imagine some of the said consequences as vividly as if they were present with him, provided that the following conditions are fulfilled: I. If the occurrence in his son's career be remarkable. II. If it be capable of being readily imagined. III. If the time of its happening be not too remote. IV. If his body be sound, in respect not only of health but of freedom from every care or business which could outwardly trouble the senses. It may also assist the result, if we think of something which generally stimulates similar ideas. For instance, if while we are talking with this or that man we hear groans, it will generally happen that, when we think of the man again, the groans heard when we spoke with him will recur to our mind. This, dear friend, is my opinion on the question you ask me. I have, I confess, been very brief, but I have furnished you with material for writing to me on the first opportunity, etc.

VOORBURG, 20 July, 1664.

SPINOZA TO BLYENBERGH.

[Spinoza answers with his usual courtesy the question propounded by Blyenbergh.]

UNKNOWN FRIEND,—I received, at Schiedam, on the 26th of December, your letter dated the 12th of December, inclosed in another written on the 24th of the same month. I gather from it your fervent love of truth, and your making it the aim of all your studies. This compelled me, though by no means otherwise unwilling, not only to grant your petition by answering all the questions you have sent, or may in future send, to the best of my ability, but also to impart to you everything in my power, which can conduce to further knowledge and sincere friendship. So far as in me lies, I value, above all other things out of my own control, the joining hands of friendship with men who are sincere lovers of truth. I believe that nothing in the world, of things outside our own control, brings more peace than the possibility of affectionate intercourse with such men; it is just as impossible that the love we bear them can be disturbed (inasmuch as it is founded on the desire each feels for the knowledge of truth), as that truth once perceived should not be assented to. It is, moreover, the highest and most pleasing source of happiness derivable from things not under our own control. Nothing save truth has power closely to unite different feelings and dispositions. I say nothing of the very great advantages which it brings, lest I should detain you too long on a subject which, doubtless, you. know already. I have said thus much, in order to show you better how gladly I shall embrace this and any future opportunity of serving you.

In order to make the best of the present opportunity, I will at once proceed to answer your question. This seems to turn on the point "that it seems to be clear, not only from God's providence, which is identical with his will, but also from God's co-operation and continuous creation of things, either that there are no such things as sin or evil, or that God directly brings sin and evil to pass." You do not, however, explain what you mean by evil. As far as one may judge from the example you give in the predetermined act of volition of Adam, you seem to mean by evil the actual exercise of volition, in so far as it is conceived as predetermined in a particular way, or in so far as it is repugnant to the command of God. Hence you conclude (and I agree with you if this be what you mean) that it is absurd to adopt either alternative, either that God brings to pass anything contrary to his own will, or that what is contrary to God's will can be good.

For my own part, I cannot admit that sin and evil have any positive existence, far' less that anything can exist, or come to pass, contrary to the will of God. On the contrary, not only do I assert that sin has no positive existence, I also maintain that only in speaking improperly, or humanly, can we say that we sin against God, as in the expression that men offend God.

As to the first point, we know that whatsoever is, when considered in itself without regard to anything else, possesses perfection, extending in each thing as far as the limits of that thing's essence: for essence is nothing else. I take for an illustration the design or determined will of Adam to eat the forbidden fruit. This design or determined will, considered in itself alone, includes perfection in so far as it expresses reality; hence it may be inferred that we can only conceive imperfection in things, when they are viewed in relation to other things possessing more reality: thus in Adam's decision, so long as we view it by itself and do not compare it with other things more perfect or exhibiting a more perfect state, we can find no imperfection: nay, it may be compared with an infinity of other things far less perfect in this respect than itself, such as stones, stocks, etc. This, as a matter of fact, everyone grants. For we all admire in animals qualities which we regard with dislike and aversion in men, such as the pugnacity of bees, the jealousy of doves, etc.; these in human beings are despised but are nevertheless considered to enhance the value of animals. This being so, it follows that sin, which indicates nothing save imperfection, cannot consist in anything that expresses reality, as we see in the case of Adam's decision and its execution.

Again, we cannot say that Adam's will is at variance with the law of God, and that it is evil because it is displeasing to God; for besides the fact that grave imperfection would be imputed to God, if we say that anything happens contrary to his will, or that he desires anything which he does not obtain, or that his nature resembled that of his creatures in having sympathy with some things more than others; such an occurrence would be at complete variance with the nature of the divine will.

The will of God is identical with his intellect; hence the former can no more be contravened than the latter, in other words, anything which should come to pass against his will must be of a nature to be contrary to his intellect, such, for instance, as a round square. Hence the will or decision of Adam regarded in itself was neither evil nor, properly speaking, against the will of God: it follows that God may — or rather, for the reason you call attention to, must — be its cause; not in so far as it was evil, for the evil in it consisted in the loss of the previous state of being which it entailed on Adam, and it is certain that loss has no positive existence, and is only so spoken of in respect to our and not God's understanding. The difficulty arises from the fact that we give one and the same definition to all the individuals of a genus, as for instance, all who have the outward appearance of men: we accordingly assume all things which are expressed by the same definition to be equally capable of attaining the highest perfection possible for the genus; when we find an individual whose actions are at variance with such perfection, we suppose him to be deprived of it, and to fall short of his nature. We should hardly act in this way, if we did not hark back to the definition and ascribe to the individual a nature in accordance with it. But as God does not know things through abstraction, or form general definitions of the kind above mentioned, and as things have no more reality than the divine understanding and power have put into them and actually endowed them with, it clearly follows that a state of privation can only be spoken of in relation to our intellect, not in relation to God.

Thus, as it seems to me, the difficulty is completely solved. However, in order to make the way still plainer, and remove every doubt, I deem it necessary to answer the two following difficulties: First, why Holy Scripture says that God wishes for the conversion of the wicked, and also why God forbade Adam to eat of the fruit when he had ordained the contrary? Secondly, that it seems to follow from what I have said, that the wicked, by their pride, avarice, and deeds of desperation, worship God in no less degree than the good do by their nobleness, patience, love, etc., inasmuch as both execute God's will.

In answer to the first question, I observe that Scripture, being chiefly fitted for and beneficial to the multitude, speaks popularly after the fashion of men. For the multitude are incapable of grasping sublime conceptions. Hence I am persuaded that all matters, which God revealed to the prophets as necessary to salvation, are set down in the form of laws. With this understanding, the prophets invented whole parables, and represented God as a king and a lawgiver, because he had revealed the means of salvation and perdition, and was their cause; the mea͏ͅ which were simply causes they styled laws and wrote th͏ͅm down as such; salvation and perdition, which are simply effects necessarily resulting from the aforesaid means, they described as reward and punishment; framing their doctrines more in accordance with such parables than with actual truth. They constantly speak of God as resembling a man, as sometimes angry, sometimes merciful, now desiring what is future, now jealous and suspicious, even as de͏ͅeived by the devil; so that philosophers and all who are above the law, that is, who follow after virtue, not in obedience to law, but through love, because it is the most excellent of all things, must not be hindered by such expressions.

Thus the command given to Adam consisted solely in this, that God revealed to Adam, that eating of the fruit brought about death; as he reveals to us, through our natural faculties, that poison is deadly. If you ask, for what object did he make this revelation, I answer in order to render Adam to that extent more perfect in knowledge. Hence, to ask God why he had not bestowed on Adam a more perfect will, is just as absurd as to ask, why the circle has not been endowed with all the properties of a sphere. This follows clearly from what has been said, and I have also proved it in my " Principles of Cartesian Philosophy," I. 15.

As to the second difficulty, it is true that the wicked execute after their manner the will of God: but they cannot, therefore, be in any respect compared with the good. The more perfection a thing has, the more does it participate in the Deity, and the more does it express perfection. Thus, as the good have incomparably more perfection than the bad, their virtue cannot be likened to the virtue of the wicked, inasmuch as the wicked lack the love of God, which proceeds from the knowledge of God, and by which alone we are, according to our human understanding, called the servants of God. The wicked, knowing not God, are but as instruments in the hand of the workman, serving unconsciously, and perishing in the using; the good, on the other hand, serve consciously, and in serving become more perfect.

This, Sir, is all I can now contribute to answering your question, and I have no higher wish than that it may satisfy you. But in case you still find any difficulty, I beg you to let me know of that also, to see if I may be able to remove it. You have nothing to fear on your side, but so long as you are not satisfied, I like nothing better than to be informed of your reasons, so that finally the truth may appear. I could have wished to write in the tongue in which I have been brought up. I should, perhaps, have been able to express my thoughts better. But be pleased to take it as it is, amend the mistakes yourself, and believe me,

Your sincere friend and servant.

Long Orchard, near Amsterdam,
    Jan. 5, 1665.

Spinoza to Blyenbergh.

[Spinoza complains that Blyenbergh has misunderstood him: he sets forth his true meaning.]

Voorburg, 28 Jan., 1665.

Friend and Sir:—When I read your first letter, I thought that our opinions almost coincided. But from the second, which was delivered to me on the 21st of this month, I see that the matter stands far otherwise, for I perceive that we disagree, not only in remote inferences from first principles, but also in first principles themselves; so that I can hardly think that we can derive

48

any mutual instruction from further correspondence. I see that no proof, though it be by the laws of proof most sound, has any weight with you, unless it agrees with the explanation, which either you yourself, or other theologians known to you, attribute to Holy Scripture. However, if you are convinced that God speaks more clearly and effectually through Holy Scripture than through the natural understanding, which he also has bestowed upon us, and with his divine wisdom keeps continually stable and uncorrupted, you have valid reasons for making your understanding bow before the opinions which you attribute to Holy Scripture; I myself could adopt no different course. For my own part, as I confess plainly, and without circumlocution, that I do not understand the Scriptures, though I have spent some years upon them, and also as I feel that when I have obtained a firm proof, I cannot fall into a state of doubt concerning it, I acquiesce entirely in what is commended to me by my understanding, without any suspicion that I am being deceived in the matter, or that Holy Scripture, though I do not search, could gainsay it: for « truth is not at variance with truth, » as I have already clearly shown in my appendix to « The Principles of Cartesian Philosophy » (I cannot give the precise reference, for I have not the book with me here in the country). But if in any instance I found that a result obtained through my natural understanding was false, I should reckon myself fortunate, for I enjoy life, and try to spend it not in sorrow and sighing, but in peace, joy, and cheerfulness, ascending from time to time a step higher. Meanwhile I know (and this knowledge gives me the highest contentment and peace of mind), that all things come to pass by the power and unchangeable decree of a Being supremely perfect.

To return to your letter, I owe you many and sincere thanks for having confided to me your philosophical opinions; but for the doctrines, which you attribute to me, and seek to infer from my letter, I return you no thanks at all. What ground, I should like to know, has my letter afforded you for ascribing to me the opinions: that men are like beasts, that they die and perish after the manner of beasts, that our actions are displeasing to God, etc.? Perhaps we are most of all at variance on this third point. You think, as far as I can judge, that God takes pleasure in our actions, as though he were a man, who has attained his object, when things fall out as he desired. For my part, have I not said plainly enough, that the good worship God, that in continually serving him they become more perfect, and that they love God? Is this, I ask, likening them to beasts, or saying that they perish like beasts, or that their actions are displeasing to God? If you had read my letter with more attention, you would have clearly perceived, that our whole dissension lies in the following alternative: Either the perfections which the good receive are imparted to them by God in his capacity of God, that is absolutely without any human qualities being ascribed to him — this is what I believe; or else such perfections are imparted by God as a judge, which is what you maintain. For this reason you defend the wicked, saying that they carry out God's decrees as far as in them lies, and therefore serve God no less than the good. · But if my doctrine be accepted, this consequence by no means follows; I do not bring in the idea of God as a judge, and, therefore I estimate an action by its intrinsic merits, not by the powers of its performer; the recompense which follows the action follows from it as necessarily as from the nature of a triangle it follows, that the three angles are equal to two right angles. This may be understood by every one who reflects on the fact, that our highest blessedness consists in love toward God, and that such love flows naturally from the knowledge of God, which is so strenuously enjoined on us. The question may very easily be proved in general terms, if we take notice of the nature of God's decrees, as explained in my appendix. However, I confess that all those, who confuse the divine nature with human nature, are gravely hindered from understanding it.

I had intended to end my letter at this point, lest I should prove troublesome to you in these questions, the discussion of which (as I discover from the extremely pious postscript added to your letter) serves you as a pastime and a jest, but for no serious use. However, that I may not summarily deny your request, I will proceed to explain further the words privation and negation, and briefly point out what is necessary for the elucidation of my former letter.

I say then, first, that PRIVATION is not the act of depriving, but simply and merely a state of want, which is in itself nothing: it is a mere entity of the reason, a mode of thought framed in comparing one thing with another. We say, for example, that a blind man is deprived of sight, because we readily imagine him as seeing, or else because we compare him with others who can see, or compare his present condition with his past condition when he could see; when we regard the man in this way, comparing his nature either with the nature of others or with his own past nature, we affirm that sight belongs to his nature, and therefore assert that he has been deprived of it. But when we are considering the nature and decree of God, we cannot affirm privation of sight in the case of the aforesaid man any more than in the case of a stone; for at the actual time sight lies no more within the scope of the man than of the stone; SINCE THERE BELONGS TO MAN AND FORMS PART OF HIS NATURE ONLY THAT WHICH IS GRANTED TO HIM BY THE UNDERSTANDING AND WILL OF GOD. Hence it follows that God is no more the cause of a blind man not seeing, than he is of a stone not seeing. Not seeing is a pure negation. SO ALSO, WHEN WE CONSIDER THE CASE OF A MAN WHO IS LED BY LUSTFUL DESIRES, WE COMPARE HIS PRESENT DESIRES WITH THOSE WHICH EXIST IN THE GOOD, OR WHICH EXISTED IN HIMSELF AT SOME OTHER TIME; WE THEN ASSERT THAT HE IS DEPRIVED OF THE BETTER DESIRES, BECAUSE WE CONCEIVE THAT VIRTUOUS DESIRES LIE WITHIN THE SCOPE OF HIS NATURE. THIS WE CANNOT DO, IF WE CONSIDER THE NATURE AND DECREE OF GOD. FOR, FROM THIS POINT OF VIEW, VIRTUOUS DESIRES LIE AT THAT TIME NO MORE WITHIN THE SCOPE OF THE NATURE OF THE LUSTFUL MAN, THAN WITHIN THE SCOPE OF THE NATURE OF THE DEVIL OR A STONE. Hence, from the latter standpoint the virtuous desire is not a privation but a negation.

Thus PRIVATION is nothing else than denying of a thing something, which we think belongs to its nature; NEGATION is denying of a thing something, which we do not think belongs to its nature.

We may now see, how Adam's desire for earthly things was evil from our standpoint, but not from God's. Although God knew both the present and the past state OF ADAM, HE DID NOT, THEREFORE, REGARD ADAM AS DEPRIVED OF HIS PAST STATE, THAT IS, HE DID NOT REGARD ADAM'S PAST STATE AS WITHIN THE SCOPE OF ADAM'S PRESENT NATURE. Otherwise God would have apprehended something contrary to his own will, that is, contrary to his own understanding. If you quite grasp my meaning here and at the same time remember, that I do not grant to the mind the same freedom as Descartes does — L[ewis] M[eyer] bears witness to this in his preface to my book — you will preceive that there is not the smallest contradiction in what I have said. But I see that I should have done far better to have answered you in my first letter with the words of Descartes, to the effect that we cannot know how our freedom and its consequences agree with the foreknowledge and freedom of God (see several passages in my appendix), that, therefore, we can discover no contradiction between creation by God and our freedom, because we cannot understand how God created the universe, nor (what is the same thing) how he preserves it. I thought that you had read the preface, and that by not giving you my real opinions in reply, I should sin against those duties of friendship which I cordially offered you. But this is of no consequence.

Still, as I see that you have not hitherto thoroughly grasped Descartes's meaning, I will call your attention to the two following points: First, that neither Descartes nor I have ever said, that it appertains to our nature to confine the will within the limits of the understanding; we have only said, that God has endowed us with a determined understanding and an undetermined will, so that we know not the object for which he has created us. Further, that an undetermined or perfect will of this kind not only makes us more perfect, but also, as I will presently show you, is extremely necessary for us.

Secondly: that our freedom is not placed in a certain contingency nor in a certain indifference, but in the method of affirmation or denial; so that, in proportion as we are less indifferent in affirmation or denial, so are we more free. For instance, if the nature of God be known to us, it follows as necessarily from our nature to affirm that God exists, as from the nature of a triangle it follows, that the three angles are equal to two right angles; we are never more free than when we affirm a thing in this way. As this necessity is nothing else but the decree of God (as I have clearly shown in my appendix), we may hence, after a fashion, understand how we act freely and are the cause of our action, though all the time we are acting necessarily and according to the decree of God. This, I repeat, we may, after a fashion, understand, whenever we affirm something, which we clearly and distinctly perceive, but when we assert something which we do not clearly and distinctly understand, in other words, when we allow our will to pass beyond the limits of our understanding, we no longer perceive the necessity nor the decree of God, we can only see our freedom which is always involved in our will; in which respect only our actions are called good or evil. If we then try to reconcile our freedom with God's decree and continuous creation, we confuse that which we clearly and distinctly understand with that which we do not perceive, and therefore, our attempt is vain. It is, therefore, sufficient for us to know that we are free, and that we can be so notwithstanding God's decree, and further that we are the cause of evil, because an act can only be called evil in relation to our freedom. I have said thus much for Descartes in order to show that, in the question we are considering, his words exhibit no contradiction.

I will now turn to what concerns myself, and will first briefly call attention to the advantage arising from my opinion, inasmuch as, according to it, our understanding

offers our mind and body to God freed from all superstition. Nor do I deny that prayer is extremely useful
to us. For my understanding is too small to determine
all the means whereby God leads men to the love of
himself, that is, to salvation. So far is my opinion from
being hurtful, that it offers to those who are not taken
up with prejudices and childish superstitions, the only
means for arriving at the highest stage of blessedness.

When you say that, by making men so dependent on
God, I reduce them to the likeness of the elements,
plants or stones, you sufficiently show that you have
thoroughly misunderstood my meaning, and have confused things which regard the understanding with things
which regard the imagination. If by your intellect only
you had perceived what dependence on God means, you
certainly would not think that things, in so far as they
depend on God are dead, corporeal, and imperfect (who
ever dared to speak so meanly of the Supremely Perfect
Being ?); on the contrary, you would understand that for
the very reason that they depend on God they are per-
~~~~; so that this dependence and necessary operation
may best be understood as God's decree, by considering,
not stocks and plants, but the most reasonable and perfect creatures. This sufficiently appears from my second
observation on the meaning of Descartes, which you
ought to have looked to.

I cannot refrain from expressing my extreme astonishment at your remarking, that if God does not punish
wrong-doing (that is, as a judge does, with a punishment not intrinsically connected with the offense, for
our whole difference lies in this), what reason prevents
me from rushing headlong into every kind of wickedness ?
Assuredly he, who is only kept from vice by the fear
of punishment (which I do not think of you), is in no
wise acted on by love, and by no means embraces virtue.
For my own part, I avoid or endeavor to avoid vice,
because it is at direct variance with my proper nature and
would lead me astray from the knowledge and love of God.

Again, if you had reflected a little on human nature
and the nature of God's decree (as explained in my

appendix), and perceived, and known by this time, how a consequence should be deduced from its premises, before a conclusion is arrived at; you would not so rashly have stated that my opinion makes us like stocks, etc.: nor would you have ascribed to me the many absurdities you conjure up.

As to the two points which you say, before passing on to your second rule, that you cannot understand; I answer, that the first may be solved through Descartes, who says that in observing your own nature you feel that you can suspend your judgment. If you say that you do not feel that you have at present sufficient force to keep your judgment suspended, this would appear to Descartes to be the same as saying that we cannot at present see, that so long as we exist we shall always be thinking things, or retain the nature of thinking things; in fact it would imply a contradiction.

As to your second difficulty, I say with Descartes, that if we cannot extend our will beyond the bounds of our extremely limited understanding, we shall be most wretched—it will not be in our power to eat even a crust of bread, or to walk a step, or to go on living, for all things are uncertain and full of peril.

I now pass on to your second rule, and assert that I believe, though I do not ascribe to Scripture that sort of truth which you think you find in it, I nevertheless assign to it as great if not greater authority than you do. I am far more careful than others not to ascribe to Scripture any childish and absurd doctrines, a precaution which demands either a thorough acquaintance with philosophy or the possession of divine revelations. Hence I pay very little attention to the glosses put upon Scripture by ordinary theologians, especially those of the kind who always interpret Scripture according to the literal and outward meaning: I have never, except among the Socinians, found any theologian stupid enough to ignore that Holy Scripture very often speaks in human fashion of God and expresses its meaning in parables; as for the contradiction which you vainly (in my opinion) endeavor to show, I think you attach to the word parable a meaning different from that usually given. For who ever heard, that a man, who expressed his opinions in parables, had therefore taken leave of his senses? When Micaiah said to King Ahab, that he had seen God sitting on a throne, with the armies of heaven standing on the right hand and the left, and that God asked his angels which of them would deceive Ahab, this was assuredly a parable employed by the prophet on that occasion (which was not fitted for the inculcation of sublime theological doctrines), as sufficiently setting forth the message he had to deliver in the name of God. We cannot say that he had in anywise taken leave of his senses. So also the other prophets of God made manifest God's commands to the people in this fashion as being the best adapted, though not expressly enjoined by God, for leading the people to the primary object of Scripture, which, as Christ himself says, is to bid men love God above all things, and ¨ neighbor as themselves. Sublime speculations have, in my opinion, no bearing on Scripture. As far as I am concerned I have never learned or been able to learn any of God's eternal attributes from Holy Scripture.

As to your fifth argument (that the prophets thus made manifest the word of God, since truth is not at variance with truth), it merely amounts, for those who understand the method of proof, to asking me to prove, that Scripture, as it is, is the true revealed word of God. The mathematical proof of this proposition could only be attained by divine revelation. I, therefore, expressed myself as follows: "I BELIEVE, BUT I DO NOT MATHEMATIC- ALLY KNOW, THAT ALL THINGS REVEALED BY GOD TO THE PROPHETS," etc. Inasmuch as I firmly believe but do not mathematically know, that the prophets were the most trusted counsellors and faithful ambassadors of God. So that in all I have written there is no contradiction, though several such may be found among holders of the opposite opinion.

The rest of your letter (to wit the passage where you say, "Lastly, the supremely perfect Being knew before- hand," etc; and again, your objections to the illustration from poison, and lastly, the whole of what you say of the appendix and what follows) seems to me beside the question.

As regards Lewis Meyer's preface, the points which were still left to be proved by Descartes before establishing his demonstration of free will, are certainly there set forth; it is added that I hold a contrary opinion, my reasons for doing so being given. I shall, perhaps, in due time, give further explanations. For the present I have no such intention.

I have never thought about the work on Descartes, nor given any further heed to it, since it has been translated into Dutch. I have my reasons, though it would be tedious to enumerate them here. So nothing remains for me but to subscribe myself, etc.

SPINOZA TO BLYENBERGH.

[Spinoza replies, that there is a difference between the theological and the philosophical way of speaking of God and things divine. He proceeds to discuss Blyenbergh's questions.]

VOORBURG, 13th March, 1665.

FRIEND AND SIR,— I have received two letters from you this week; the second, dated 9th March, only served to inform me of the first written on February 19th, and sent to me at Schiedam. In the former I see that you complain of my saying, that "demonstration carried no weight with you," as though I had spoken of my own arguments which had failed to convince you. Such was far from my intention. I was referring to your own words, which ran as follows:—"And if after long investigation it comes to pass, that my natural knowledge appears either to be at variance with the word (of Scripture), or not sufficiently well, etc.; the word has so great authority with me, that I would rather doubt of the conceptions, which I think I clearly perceive," etc. You see I merely repeat in brief your own phrase, so that I cannot think you have any cause for anger against me, especially as I merely quoted in order to show the great difference between our standpoints.

Again, as you wrote at the end of your letter that

your only hope and wish is to continue in faith and hope, and that all else, which we may become convinced of through our natural faculties, is indifferent to you; I reflected, as I still continue to do, that my letters could be of no use to you, and that I should best consult my own interests by ceasing to neglect my pursuits (which I am compelled while writing to you to interrupt) for the sake of things which could bring no possible benefit. Nor is this contrary to the spirit of my former letter, for in that I looked upon you as simply a philosopher, who (like not a few who call themselves Christians) possesses no touchstone of truth save his natural understanding, and not as a theologian. However, you have taught me to know better, and have also shown me that the foundation, on which I was minded to build up our friendship, has not, as I imagined, been laid.

As for the rest, such are the general accompaniments of controversy, so that I would not on that account transgress the limits of courtesy: I will, therefore, pass over in your second letter, and in this, these and similar expressions, as though they had never been observed. So much for your taking offense; to show you that I have given you no just cause, and, also, that I am quite willing to brook contradiction. I now turn a second time to answering your objections.

I maintain, in the first place, that God is absolutely and really the cause of all things which have essence, whatsoever they may be. If you can demonstrate that evil, error, crime, etc., have any positive existence, which expresses essence, I will fully grant you that God is the cause of crime, evil, error, etc. I believe myself to have sufficiently shown, that that which constitutes the reality of evil, error, crime, etc., does not consist in anything, which expresses essence, and therefore we cannot say that God is its cause. For instance, Nero's matricide, in so far as it comprehended anything positive, was not a crime; the same outward act was perpetrated, and the same matricidal intention was entertained by Orestes; who, nevertheless, is not blamed — at any rate not so much as Nero. Wherein, then, did Nero's crime consist?

In nothing else, but that by his deed he showed himself to be ungrateful, unmerciful, and disobedient. Certainly none of these qualities express aught of essence, therefore, God was not the cause of them, though he was the cause of Nero's act and intention.

Further, I would have you observe, that, while we speak philosophically, we ought not to employ theological phrases. For, since theology frequently, and not unwisely, represents God as a perfect man, it is often expedient in theology to say, that God desires a given thing, that he is angry at the actions of the wicked, and delights in those of the good. But in philosophy, when we clearly perceive that the attributes which make men perfect can as ill be ascribed and assigned to God, as the attributes which go to make perfect the elephant and the ass can be ascribed to man; here I say these and similar phrases have no place, nor can we employ them without causing extreme confusion in our conceptions. Hence, in the language of philosophy, it cannot be said that God desires anything of any man, or that anything is displeasing or pleasing to him: all these are human qualities and have no place in God.

I would have it observed, that although the actions of the good (that is, of those who have a clear idea of God, whereby all their actions and their thoughts are determined) and of the wicked (that is, of those who do not possess the idea of God, but only the ideas of earthly things, whereby their actions and thoughts are determined), and, in fact, of all things that are, necessarily flow from God's eternal laws and decrees; yet they do not differ from one another in degree only, but also in essence. A mouse no less than an angel, and sorrow no less than joy depend on God; yet a mouse is not a kind of angel, neither is sorrow a kind of joy. I think I have thus answered your objections, if I rightly understand them, for I sometimes doubt, whether the conclusions which you deduce are not foreign to the proposition you are undertaking to prove.

However, this will appear more clearly, if I answer the questions you proposed on these principles. First,

Whether murder is as acceptable to God as almsgiving? Secondly, Whether stealing is as good in relation to God as honesty? Thirdly and lastly, Whether if there be a mind so framed, that it would agree with, rather than be repugnant to its proper nature, to give way to lust, and to commit crimes, whether, I repeat, there can be any reason given, why such a mind should do good and eschew evil?

To your first question, I answer, that I do not know, speaking as a philosopher, what you mean by the words "acceptable to God." If you ask, whether God does not hate the wicked and love the good? whether God does not regard the former with dislike, and the latter with favor? I answer, No. If the meaning of your question is: Are murderers and almsgivers equally good and perfect? my answer is again in the negative. To your second question, I reply: If, by "good in relation to God," you mean that the honest man confers a favor on God, and the thief does him an injury, I answer that neither the honest man nor the thief can cause God any pleasure or displeasure. If you mean to ask, whether the actions of each, in so far as they possess reality, and are caused by God, are equally perfect? I reply that, if we merely regard the actions and the manner of their execution, both may be equally perfect. If you, therefore, inquire whether the thief and the honest man are equally perfect and blessed? I answer, No. For, by an honest man, I mean one who always desires that everyone should possess that which is his. This desire, as I prove in my "Ethics" (as yet unpublished), necessarily derives its origin in the pious from the clear knowledge which they possess of God and of themselves. As a thief has no desire of the kind, he is necessarily without the knowledge of God and of himself—in other words, without the chief element of our blessedness. If you further ask, What causes you to perform a given action, which I call virtuous, rather than another? I reply, that I cannot know which method, out of the infinite methods at his disposal, God employs to determine you to the said action. It may be, that God has impressed you with a clear idea of himself, so that you forget the world for love of him, and love your fellow-men as yourself; it is plain that such a disposition is at variance with those dispositions which are called bad, and, therefore, could not co-exist with them in the same man.

However, this is not the place to expound all the foundations of my "Ethics," or to prove all that I have advanced; I am now only concerned in answering your questions, and defending myself against them.

Lastly, as to your third question, it assumes a contradiction, and seems to me to be, as though one asked: If it agreed better with a man's nature that he should hang himself, could any reasons be given for his not hanging himself? Can such a nature possibly exist? If so, I maintain (whether I do or do not grant free will), that such an one, if he sees that he can live more conveniently on the gallows than sitting at his own table, would act most foolishly, if he did not hang himself. So anyone who clearly saw that, by committing crimes, he would enjoy a really more perfect and better life and existence, than he could attain by the practice of virtue, would be foolish if he did not act on his convictions. For, with such a perverse human nature as his, crime would become virtue.

As to the other question, which you add in your postscript, seeing that one might ask a hundred such in an hour, without arriving at a conclusion about any, and seeing that you yourself do not press for an answer, I will send none.

I will now only subscribe myself, etc.

Spinoza to Blyenbergh

[Spinoza declines further correspondence with Blyenbergh, but says he will give explanations of certain points by word of mouth. (Voorburg, 3d June, 1665.)]

FRIEND AND SIR,—When your letter, dated 27th March, was delivered to me, I was just starting for Amsterdam. I, therefore, after reading half of it, left it at home, to be answered on my return: for I thought it dealt only with questions raised in our first controversy. However, a second perusal showed me, that it embraced a far wider subject, and not only asked me for proof of what, in my preface to "Principles of Cartesian Philosophy," I wrote (with the object of merely stating, without proving or urging my opinion), but also requested me to impart a great portion of my "Ethics," which, as everyone knows, ought to be based on physics and metaphysics. For this reason, I have been unable to allow myself to satisfy your demands. I wished to await an opportunity for begging you, in a most friendly way, by word of mouth, to withdraw your request, for giving you my reasons for refusal, and for showing that your inquiries do not promote the solution of our first controversy, but, on the contrary, are for the most part entirely dependent on its previous settlement. So far are they not essential to the understanding of my doctrine concerning necessity, that they cannot be apprehended, unless the latter question is understood first. However, before such an opportunity offered, a second letter reached me this week, appearing to convey a certain sense of displeasure at my delay. Necessity, therefore, has compelled me to write you these few words, to acquaint you more fully with my proposal and decision. I hope that, when the facts of the case are before you, you will, of your own accord, desist from your request, and will still remain kindly disposed toward me. I, for my part, will, in all things, according to my power, prove myself your, etc.

Spinoza to Christian Huyghens.

[Treating of the Unity of God.]

Distinguished Sir,—The demonstration of the unity of God on the ground that his nature involves necessary existence, which you asked for, and I took note of, I have been prevented by various business from sending to you before. In order to accomplish my purpose, I will premise:—

I. That the true definition of anything includes nothing except the simple nature of the thing defined. From this it follows:—

II. That no definition can involve or express a multitude or a given number of individuals, inasmuch as it involves and expresses nothing except the nature of the thing as it is in itself. For instance, the definition of a triangle includes nothing beyond the simple nature of a triangle; it does not include any given number of triangles. In like manner, the definition of the mind as a thinking thing, or the definition of God as a perfect being, includes nothing beyond the natures of the mind and of God, not a given number of minds or gods.

III. That for everything that exists there must necessarily be a positive cause, through which it exists.

IV. This cause may be situate either in the nature and definition of the thing itself (to wit, because existence belongs to its nature or necessarily includes it), or externally to the thing.

From these premises it follows, that if any given number of individuals exists in nature, there must be one or more causes, which have been able to produce exactly that number of individuals, neither more nor less. If, for instance, there existed in nature twenty men (in order to avoid all confusion, I will assume that these all exist together as primary entities), it is not enough to investigate the cause of human nature in general, in order to account for the existence of these twenty; we must also inquire into the reason, why there exist exactly twenty men, neither more nor less. For (by our third hypothesis) for each man a reason and a cause must be forthcoming, why he should exist. But this cause (by our second and third hypotheses) cannot be contained in the nature of man himself; for the true definition of man does not involve the number of twenty men. Hence (by our fourth hypothesis) the cause for the existence of these twenty men, and consequently for the existence of each of them, must exist externally to them. We may thus absolutely conclude, that all things, which are conceived to exist in the plural number, must necessarily be produced by external causes and not by the force of their own nature. But since (by our second hypothesis) necessary existence appertains to the nature of God, his true definition must necessarily include necessary existence: therefore from his true definition his necessary existence must be inferred. But from his true definition (as I have already demonstrated from our second and third hypotheses) the necessary existence of many gods cannot be inferred. Therefore there only follows the existence of a single God. Which was to be proved.

This, distinguished sir, has now seemed to me the best method for demonstrating the proposition. I have also proved it differently by means of the distinction between essence and existence; but bearing in mind the object you mentioned to me, I have preferred to send you the demonstration given above. I hope it will satisfy you, and I will await your reply, meanwhile remaining, etc.

VOORBURG, 7 Jan. 1666.

SPINOZA TO CHRISTIAN HUYGHENS.

(Further arguments for the unity of God.)

DISTINGUISHED SIR:— In your last letter, written on March 30th, you have excellently elucidated the point, which was somewhat obscure to me in your letter of February 10th. As I now know your opinion, I will set forth the state of the question as you conceive it; whether there be only a single being who subsists by his own sufficiency or force? I not only affirm this to be so, but also undertake to prove it from the fact, that the nature of such a being necessarily involves existence; perhaps it may also be readily proved from the understanding of God (as I set forth, "Principles of Cartesian Philosophy," I. Prop. i.), or from others of his attributes. Before treating of the subject I will briefly show, as preliminaries, what properties must be possessed by a being including necessary existence. To wit:

I. It must be eternal. For if a definite duration be assigned to it, it would beyond that definite duration be conceived as non-existent, or as not involving necessary existence, which would be contrary to its definition.

II. It must be simple, not made up of parts. For parts must in nature and knowledge be prior to the whole they compose: this could not be the case with regard to that which is eternal.

III. It cannot be conceived as determinate, but only as infinite. For, if the nature of the said being were determinate, and conceived as determinate, that nature would beyond the said limits be conceived as non-existent, which again is contrary to its definition.

IV. It is indivisible. For if it were divisible, it could be divided into parts, either of the same or of different nature. If the latter, it could be destroyed and so not exist, which is contrary to its definition; if the former, each part would in itself include necessary existence, and thus one part could exist without others, and consequently be conceived as so existing. Hence the nature of the being would be comprehended as finite, which, by what has been said, is contrary to its definition. Thus we see that in attempting to ascribe to such a being any imperfection, we straightway fall into contradictions. For, whether the imperfection which we wish to assign to the said being be situate in any defect, or in limitations possessed by its nature, or in any change which it might, through deficiency of power, undergo from external causes, we are always brought back to the contradiction, that a nature which involves necessary existence, does not exist, or does not necessarily exist. I conclude, therefore—

V. That everything, which includes necessary existence, cannot have in itself any imperfection, but must express pure perfection.

VI. Further, since only from perfection can it come about, that any being should exist by its own sufficiency and force, it follows that, if we assume a being to exist by its own nature, but not to express all perfections, we must further suppose that another being exists, which does comprehend in itself all perfections. For, if the less powerful being exists by its own sufficiency, how much more must the more powerful so exist?

Lastly, to deal with the question, I affirm that there can only be a single being, of which the existence belongs to its nature; such a being which possesses in itself all perfections I will call God. If there be any being to whose nature existence belongs, such a being can contain in itself no imperfection, but must (by my fifth premise) express every perfection; therefore, the nature of such a being seems to belong to God (whose existence we are bound to affirm by Premise VI.), inasmuch as he has in himself all perfections and no imperfections. Nor can it exist externally to God. For if, externally to God, there existed one and the same nature involving necessary existence, such nature would be twofold; but this, by what we have just shown, is absurd. Therefore there is nothing save God, but there is a single God, that involves necessary existence, which was to be proved.

Such, distinguished sir, are the arguments I can now produce for demonstrating this question. I hope I may also demonstrate to you, that I am, etc.

Voorburg, 10 April, 1666.

Spinoza to Christian Huyghens.

[Further discussion concerning the unity of God. Spinoza asks for advice about polishing lenses. (Voorburg, May, 1666.)]

Distinguished Sir:— I have been by one means or another prevented from answering sooner your letter, dated May 19th. As I gather that you suspend your judgment with regard to most of the demonstration I sent you (owing, I believe, to the obscurity you find in it), I will here endeavor to explain its meaning more clearly.

First, I enumerated four properties, which a being existing by its own sufficiency or force must possess. These four, and others like them, I reduced in my fifth observation to one. Further, in order to deduce all things necessary for the demonstration from a single premise, I endeavored in my sixth observation to demonstrate the existence of God from the given hypothesis; whence, lastly, taking (as you know) nothing beyond the ordinary meaning of the terms, I drew the desired conclusion.

Such, in brief, was my purpose and such my aim. I will now explain the meaning of each step singly, and will first start with the aforesaid four properties.

In the first you find no difficulty, nor is it anything but, as in the case of the second, an axiom. By simple I merely mean not compound, or not made up of parts differing in nature or other parts agreeing in nature. This demonstration is assuredly universal.

The sense of my third observation (that if the being be thought, it cannot be conceived as limited by thought, but only as infinite, and similarly, if it be extension, it cannot be conceived as limited by extension) you have excellently perceived, though you say you do not perceive the conclusion; this last is based on the fact, that a contradiction is involved in conceiving under the category of non-existence anything, whose definition includes or (what is the same thing) affirms existence. And since determination implies nothing positive, but only a limitation of the existence of the nature conceived as determinate, it follows that, that of which the definition affirms existence, cannot be conceived as determinate. For instance, if the term extension included necessary existence, it would be alike impossible to conceive extension without existence and existence without extension. If this were established, it would be impossible to conceive determinate extension. For, if it be conceived as determinate, it must be determined by its own nature, that is by extension, and this extension, whereby it is determined, must be conceived under the category of non-existence, which by the hypothesis is obviously a contradiction. In my fourth observation, I merely wished to show, that such a being could neither be divided into parts of the same nature or parts of a different nature, whether those of a different nature involve necessary existence or not. If, I said, we adopt the second view, the being would be destroyed; for destruction is merely the resolution of a thing into parts so that none of them expresses the nature of the whole; if we adopt the first view, we should be in contradiction with the first three properties.

In my fifth observation, I merely asserted, that perfection consists in being, and imperfection in the privation of being. I say the privation; for although extension denies of itself thought, this argues no imperfection in it. It would be an imperfection in it, if it were in any degree deprived of extension, as it would be, if it were determinate; or again, if it lacked duration, position, etc.

My sixth observation you accept absolutely, and yet you say, that your whole difficulty remains (inasmuch as there may be, you think, several self-existent entities of different nature; as for instance thought and extension are different and perhaps subsist by their own sufficiency). I am, therefore, forced to believe, that you attribute to my observation a meaning quite different from the one intended by me. I think I can discern your interpretation of it; however, in order to save time, I will merely set forth my own meaning. I say then, as regards my sixth observation, that if we assert that anything, which is indeterminate and perfect only after its kind, exists by its own sufficiency, we must also grant the existence of a Being indeterminate and perfect absolutely; such a Being I will call God. If, for example, we wish to assert that extension or thought (which are each perfect after their kind, that is, in a given sphere of being) exists by its own sufficiency, we must grant also the existence of God, who is absolutely perfect, that is, of a Being absolutely indeterminate. I would here direct attention to what I have just said with regard to the term IMPERFECTION; namely, that it signifies that a thing is deficient in some quality, which, nevertheless, belongs to its nature. For instance, extension can only be called imperfect in respect of duration, position, or quantity: that is, as not enduring longer, as not retaining its position, or as not

Massacre of the last Jews of England in 1190.

Not until 1656 were Jews readmitted to England, largely upon the appeal to Cromwell of Menasseh ben Israel, Spinoza's teacher.

being greater. It can never be called imperfect, because it does not think, inasmuch as its nature requires nothing of the kind, but consists solely in extension, that is in a certain sphere of being. Only in respect to its own sphere can it be called determinate or indeterminate, perfect or imperfect. Now, since the nature of God is not confined to a certain sphere of being, but exists in being, which is absolutely indeterminate, so his nature also demands everything which perfectly expresses being; otherwise his nature would be determinate and deficient.

This being so, it follows that there can be only one Being, namely God, who exists by his own force. If, for the sake of an illustration, we assert, that extension involves existence, it is, therefore, necessary that it should be eternal and indeterminate, and express absolutely no imperfection, but perfection. Hence extension will appertain to God, or will be something which in some fashion expresses the nature of God, since God is a Being, who not only in a certain respect but absolutely is in essence indeterminate and omnipotent. What we have here said by way of illustration regarding extension must be asserted of all that we ascribe a similar existence to. I, therefore, conclude as in my former letter, that there is nothing external to God, but that God alone exists by his own sufficiency. I think I have said enough to show the meaning of my former letter; however, of this you will be the best judge. . .

(The rest of the letter is occupied with details about the polishing of lenses.)

SPINOZA TO I. BRESSER (JUNE, 1665).

[Spinoza urges his correspondent to be diligent in studying philosophy, promises to send part of the «Ethics,» and adds some personal details.]

DEAR FRIEND,— I do not know whether you have quite forgotten me; but there are many circumstances which lead me to suspect it. First, when I was setting out on my journey, I wished to bid you good-bye; and, after your own invitation, thinking I should certainly find you at home, heard that you had gone to The Hague. I return to Voorburg, nothing doubting but that you would at least have visited me in passing; but you, forsooth, without greeting your friend, went back home. Three weeks have I waited, without getting sight of a letter from you. If you wish this opinion of mine to be changed, you may easily change it by writing; and you can at the same time, point out a means of entering into a correspondence, as we once talked of doing at your house.

Meanwhile, I should like to ask you, nay I do beg and entreat you, by our friendship, to apply yourself to some serious work with real study, and to devote the chief part of your life to the cultivation of your understanding and your soul. Now, while there is time, and before you complain of having let time and, indeed, your own self slip by. Further, in order to set our correspondence on foot, and to give you courage to write to me more freely, I would have you know that I have long thought, and, indeed, been almost certain, that you are somewhat too diffident of your own abilities, and that you are afraid of advancing some question or proposal unworthy of a man of learning. It does not become me to praise you, and expatiate on your talents to your face; but, if you are afraid that I shall show your letters to others, who will laugh at you, I give you my word of honor, that I will religiously keep them, and will show them to no mortal without your leave. On these conditions, you may enter on a correspondence, unless you doubt of my good faith, which I do not in the least believe. I want to hear your opinion on this in your first letter; and you may, at the same time, send me the conserve of red roses, though I am now much better.

After my journey, I was once bled; but the fever did not cease, though I was somewhat more active than before the bleeding, owing, I think, to the change of air; but I was two or three times laid up with a tertian. This, however, by good diet, I have at length driven away, and sent about its business. Where it has gone,

I know not; but I am taking care it does not return here.

As regards the third part of my philosophy, I will shortly send it you, if you wish to be its transmitter, or to our friend De Vries; and, although I had settled not to send any of it, till it was finished, yet as it takes longer than I thought, I am unwilling to keep you waiting. I will send up to the eightieth proposition, or thereabouts.

Of English affairs I hear a good deal, but nothing for certain. The people continue to be apprehensive, and can see no reason, why the fleet should not be despatched; but the matter does not yet seem to be set on foot. I am afraid our rulers want to be overwise and prudent; but the event will show what they intend, and what they will attempt. May the gods turn it all to good. I want to know what our people think, where you are, and what they know for certain; but, above all things, I want you to believe me, etc.

SPINOZA TO I. BRESSER (JUNE, 1665).

[Concerning the best method, by which we may safely arrive at the knowledge of things.]

MOST LEARNED SIR AND DEAREST FRIEND,— I have not been able hitherto to answer your last letter, received some time back. I have been so hindered by various occupations and calls on my time, that I am hardly yet free from them. However, as I have a few spare moments, I do not want to fall short of my duty, but take this first opportunity of heartily thanking you for your affection and kindness toward me, which you have often displayed in your actions, and now also abundantly prove by your letter.

I pass on to your question, which runs as follows: " Is there, or can there be, any method by which we may, without hindrance, arrive at the knowledge of the most excellent things ? or are our minds, like our bodies, subject to the vicissitudes of circumstance, so that our thoughts are governed rather by fortune than by skill ? " I think I shall satisfy you, if I show that there must necessarily be a method, whereby we are able to direct our clear and distinct perceptions, and that our mind is not, like our body, subject to the vicissitudes of circumstance.

This conclusion may be based simply on the consideration that one clear and distinct perception, or several such together, can be absolutely the cause of another clear and distinct perception. Now, all the clear and distinct perceptions, which we form, can only arise from other clear and distinct perceptions, which are in us; nor do they acknowledge any cause external to us. Hence it follows that the clear and distinct perceptions, which we form, depend solely on our nature, and on its certain and fixed laws; in other words, on our absolute power, not on fortune — that is, not on causes which, although also acting by certain and fixed laws, are yet unknown to us, and alien to our nature and power. As regards other perceptions, I confess that they depend chiefly on fortune. Hence clearly appears, what the true method ought to be like, and what it ought chiefly to consist in — namely, solely in the knowledge of the pure understanding, and its nature and laws. In order that such knowledge may be acquired, it is before all things necessary to distinguish between the understanding and the imagination, or between ideas which are true and the rest, such as the fictitious, the false, the doubtful, and absolutely all which depend solely on the memory. For the understanding of these matters, as far as the method requires, there is no need to know the nature of the mind through its first cause; it is sufficient to put together a short history of the mind, or of perceptions, in the manner taught by Verulam.

I think that in these few words I have explained and demonstrated the true method, and have, at the same time, pointed out the way of acquiring it. It only remains to remind you, that all these questions demand assiduous study, and great firmness of disposition and purpose. In order to fulfil these conditions, it is of prime necessity to follow a fixed mode and plan of living, and to set before one some definite aim. But enough of this for the present, etc.

[Spinoza begs his friend to stop the printing of the Dutch version of the «Tractatus Theologico-Politicus.» Some remarks on a pernicious pamphlet, « Homo Politicus,» and on Thales of Miletus.]

MOST COURTEOUS SIR,—When Professor N. N. visited me the other day, he told me that my "Theologico-Political Treatise" has been translated into Dutch, and that someone whose name he did not know, was about printing it. With regard to this, I earnestly beg you to inquire carefully into the business, and, if possible, stop the printing. This is the request not only of myself, but of many of my friends and acquaintances, who would be sorry to see the book placed under an interdict, as it undoubtedly would be, if published in Dutch. I do not doubt, but that you will do this service to me and the cause.

One of my friends sent me a short time since a pamphlet called "Homo Politicus," of which I had heard much. I have read it, and find it to be the most pernicious work which man could devise or invent. Rank and riches are the author's highest good; he adapts his doctrine accordingly, and shows the means to acquire them; to wit, by inwardly rejecting all religion, and outwardly professing whatever best serves his own advancement, also by keeping faith with no one, except in so far as he himself is profited thereby. For the rest, to feign, to make promises and break them, to lie, to swear falsely, and many such like practices call forth his highest praises. When I had finished reading the book, I debated whether I should write a pamphlet indirectly aimed against its author, wherein I should treat of the highest good and show the troubled and wretched condition of those who are covetous of rank and riches; finally proving by very plain reasoning and many examples, that the insatiable desire for rank and riches must bring and has brought ruin to states.

How much better and more excellent than the doctrines of the aforesaid writer are the reflections of Thales of Miletus, appears from the following: All the goods of friends, he says, are in common; wise men are the friends of the gods, and all things belong to the gods; therefore all things belong to the wise. Thus in a single sentence this wisest of men accounts himself most rich, rather by nobly despising riches than by sordidly seeking them. In other passages he shows that the wise lack riches, not from necessity, but from choice. For when his friends reproached him with his poverty he answered, " Do you wish me to show you, that I could acquire what I deem unworthy of my labor, but you so diligently seek ? " On their answering in the affirmative, he hired every oil-press in the whole of Greece (for being a distinguished astrologer he knew that the olive harvest would be as abundant as in previous years it had been scanty), and sub-let at his own price what he had hired for a very small sum, thus acquiring in a single year a large fortune, which he bestowed liberally as he had gained it industriously, etc.

THE HAGUE, 17 Feb., 1671.

SPINOZA TO ISAAC OROBIO.

[A defense of the " Tractatus Theologico-Politicus." (The Hague, 1671.)]

MOST LEARNED SIR,— You doubtless wonder why I have kept you so long waiting. I could hardly bring myself to reply to the pamphlet of that person, which you thought fit to send me; indeed I only do so now because of my promise. However, in order as far as possible to humor my feelings, I will fulfill my engagement in as few words as I can, and will briefly show how perversely he has interpreted my meaning; whether through malice or through ignorance I cannot readily say. But to the matter in hand.

First he says, " THAT IT IS OF LITTLE MOMENT TO KNOW WHAT NATION I BELONG TO, OR WHAT SORT OF LIFE I LEAD." Truly, if he had known, he would not so easily have persuaded himself that I teach Atheism. For Atheists are wont greedily to covet rank and riches, which I have always despised, as all who know me are aware. Again, in order to smooth his path to the object he has in view, he says that, "I AM POSSESSED OF NO MEAN TALENTS," so that he may, forsooth, more easily convince his readers, that I have knowingly and cunningly with evil intent argued for the cause of the deists, in order to discredit it. This contention sufficiently shows that he has not understood my reasons. For who could be so cunning and clever, as to be able to advance under false pretenses so many and such good reasons for a doctrine which he did not believe in? Who will pass for an honest writer in the eyes of a man, that thinks one may argue as soundly for fiction as for truth? But after all I am not astonished. Descartes was formerly served in the same way by Voët, and the most honorable writers are constantly thus treated.

He goes on to say, "IN ORDER TO SHUN THE REPROACH OF SUPERSTITION, HE SEEMS TO ME TO HAVE THROWN OFF ALL RELIGION." What this writer means by religion and what by superstition, I know not. But I would ask, whether a man throws off all religion, who maintains that God must be acknowledged as the highest good, and must, as such, be loved with a free mind? or, again, that the reward of virtue is virtue itself, while the punishment of folly and weakness is folly itself? or, lastly, that every man ought to love his neighbor, and to obey the commands of the supreme power? Such doctrines I have not only expressly stated, but have also demonstrated them by very solid reasoning. However, I think I see the mud wherein this person sticks. He finds nothing in virtue and the understanding in themselves to please him, but would prefer to live in accordance with his passions, if it were not for the single obstacle that he fears punishment. He abstains from evil actions, and obeys the divine commands like a slave, with unwillingness and hesitation, expecting as the reward of his bondage to be recompensed by God with gifts far more pleasing than divine love, and greater in proportion to his dislike to goodness and consequent unwillingness to practice it. Hence it comes to pass, that he believes that all, who are not restrained by this fear, lead a life of license and throw off all religion. But this I pass over, and proceed to the deduction, whereby he wishes to show, that "WITH COVERT AND DISGUISED ARGUMENTS I TEACH ATHEISM." The foundation of his reasoning is, that he thinks I take away freedom from God, and subject him to fate. This is flatly false. For I have maintained, that all things follow by inevitable necessity from the nature of God, in the same way as all maintain that it follows from the nature of God, that he understands himself: no one denies that this latter consequence follows necessarily from the divine nature, yet no one conceives that God is constrained by any fate; they believe that he understands himself with entire freedom, though necessarily. I find nothing here, that cannot be perceived by every one; if, nevertheless, my adversary thinks that these arguments are advanced with evil intent, what does he think of his own Descartes, who asserted that nothing is done by us, which has not been pre-ordained by God, nay, that we are newly created as it were by God every moment, though none the less we act according to our own free will? This, as Descartes himself confesses, no one can understand.

Further, this inevitable necessity in things destroys neither divine laws nor human. For moral principles, whether they have received from God the form of laws or not, are nevertheless divine and salutary. Whether we accept the good, which follows from virtue and the divine love, as given us by God as a judge, or as emanating from the necessity of the divine nature, it is not in either case more or less to be desired; nor are the evils which follow from evil actions less to be feared, because they follow necessarily: finally, whether we act under necessity or freedom, we are in either case led by hope and fear. Wherefore the assertion is false, "THAT I MAINTAIN THAT THERE IS NO ROOM LEFT FOR PRECEPTS AND COMMANDS." Or as he goes on to say, "THAT THERE IS NO EXPECTATION OF REWARD OR PUNISHMENT, SINCE ALL THINGS ARE ASCRIBED TO FATE, AND ARE SAID TO FLOW WITH INEVITABLE NECESSITY FROM GOD."

I do not here inquire, why it is the same, or almost the

same to say that all things necessarily flow from God, as to say that God is universal; but I would have you observe the insinuation which he not less maliciously subjoins, " THAT I WISH THAT MEN SHOULD PRACTICE VIRTUE, NOT BECAUSE OF THE PRECEPTS AND LAW OF GOD, OR THROUGH HOPE OF REWARD AND FEAR OF PUNISHMENT, BUT," etc. Such a sentiment you will assuredly not find anywhere in my treatise: on the contrary, I have expressly stated in Chap. IV., that the sum of the divine law (which, as I have said in Chap. II., has been divinely inscribed on our hearts), and its chief precept is, to love God as the highest good: not, indeed, from the fear of any punishment, for love cannot spring from fear; nor for the love of anything which we desire for our own delight, for then we should love not God, but the object of our desire.

I have shown in the same chapter, that God revealed this law to the prophets, so that, whether it received from God the form of a command, or whether we conceive it to be like God's other decrees, which involve eternal necessity and truth, it will in either case remain God's decree and a salutary principle. Whether I love God in freedom, or whether I love him from the necessity of the divine decree, I shall nevertheless love God, and shall be in a state of salvation. Wherefore, I can now declare here, that this person is one of that sort, of whom I have said at the end of my preface, that I would rather that they utterly neglected my book, than that by misinterpreting it after their wont, they should become hostile, and hinder others without benefiting themselves.

Though I think I have said enough to prove what I intended, I have yet thought it worth while to add a few observations—namely, that this person falsely thinks, that I have in view the axiom of theologians, which draws a distinction between the words of a prophet when propounding doctrine, and the same prophet when narrating an event. If by such an axiom he means that which in Chap. XV. I attributed to a certain R. Jehuda Alpakhar, how could he think that I agree with it, when in that very chapter I reject it as false? If he does not mean this, I confess I am as yet in ignorance as to what he does mean, and, therefore, could not have had it in view.

Again, I cannot see why he says, that all will adopt my opinions, who deny that reason and philosophy should be the interpreters of Scripture; I have refuted the doctrine of such persons, together with that of Maimonides.

It would take too long to review all the indications he gives of not having judged me altogether calmly. I therefore pass on to his conclusion where he says, "THAT I HAVE NO ARGUMENTS LEFT TO PROVE, THAT MAHOMET WAS NOT A TRUE PROPHET." This he endeavors to show from my opinions, whereas from them it clearly follows, that Mahomet was an impostor, inasmuch as he utterly forbids that freedom, which the Catholic religion revealed by our natural faculties and by the prophets grants, and which I have shown should be granted in its completeness. Even if this were not so, am I, I should like to know, bound to show that any prophet is false? Surely the burden lies with the prophets, to prove that they are true. But if he retorts that Mahomet also taught the divine law, and gave certain signs of his mission, as the rest of the prophets did, there is surely no reason why he should deny that Mahomet also was a true prophet.

As regards the Turks and other non-Christian nations; if they worship God by the practice of justice and charity toward their neighbor, I believe that they have the spirit of Christ, and are in a state of salvation, whatever they may ignorantly hold with regard to Mahomet and oracles.

Thus you see, my friend, how far this man has strayed from the truth; nevertheless, I grant that he has inflicted the greatest injury, not on me, but on himself, inasmuch as he has not been ashamed to declare, that "UNDER DISGUISED AND COVERT ARGUMENTS I TEACH ATHEISM."

I do not think, that you will find any expressions I have used against this man too severe. However, if there be any of the kind which offend you, I beg you to correct them as you shall think fit. I have no disposition to irritate him, whoever he may be, and to raise

The burning of Jews in the process of the Inquisition had a profound influence upon Spinoza's thinking.

up by my labors enemies against myself; as this is often
the result of disputes like the present, I could scarcely
prevail on myself to reply—nor should I have prevailed,
if I had not promised. Farewell. I commit to your pru-
dence this letter, and myself, who am, etc.

SPINOZA TO JARIG JELLIS.

[Of the difference between the political theories of Hobbes and
Spinoza, of the Unity of God, of the notion of figure, of the book
of a Utrecht professor against the "Tractatus Theologico-Politicus."]

MOST COURTEOUS SIR,—As regards political theories,
the difference which you inquire about between Hobbes
and myself, consists in this, that I always preserve natural
right intact, and only allot to the chief magistrates in
every state a right over their subjects commensurate
with the excess of their power over the power of the
subjects. This is what always takes place in the state
of nature.

Again, with regard to the demonstration which I establish in the appendix to my geometric exposition of Cartesian principles, namely, that God can only with great
impropriety be called one or single, I answer that a
thing can only be called one or single in respect of existence, not in respect of essence. For we do not conceive
things under the category of numbers, unless they have
first been reduced to a common genus. For example, he
who holds in his hand a penny and a crownpiece will
not think of the twofold number, unless he can call
both the penny and the crownpiece by one and the same
name, to wit, coins or pieces of money. In the latter
case he can say that he holds two coins or pieces of
money, inasmuch as he calls the crown as well as the
penny, a coin, or piece of money. Hence, it is evident
that a thing cannot be called one or single, unless there
be afterward another thing conceived, which (as has
been said) agrees with it. Now, since the existence of
God is his essence, and of his essence we can form no

general idea, it is certain, that he who calls God one or single has no true idea of God, and speaks of him very improperly.

As to the doctrine that figure is negation and not anything positive, it is plain that the whole of matter considered indefinitely can have no figure, and that figure can only exist in finite and determinate bodies. For he who says, that he perceives a figure, merely indicates thereby, that he conceives a determinate thing, and how it is determinate. This determination, therefore, does not appertain to the thing according to its being, but, on the contrary, is its non-being. As then figure is nothing else than determination, and determination is negation, figure, as has been said, can be nothing but negation.

The book, which a Utrecht professor wrote against mine, and which was published after his death, I saw lying in a bookseller's window. From the little I then read of it, I judged it unworthy of perusal, still less of reply. I, therefore, left the book, and its author. With an inward smile I reflected, that the most ignorant are ever the most audacious and the most ready to rush into print. The Christians seem to me to expose their wares for sale like hucksters, who always show first that which is worst. The devil is said to be very cunning, but to my thinking the tricks of these people are in cunning far beyond his. Farewell.

THE HAGUE, 2 June, 1674.

SPINOZA TO LEIBNIZ.

MOST LEARNED AND DISTINGUISHED SIR,—I have read the paper you were kind enough to send me, and return you many thanks for the communication. I regret that I have not been able quite to follow your meaning, though you explain it sufficiently clearly, whether you think that there is any cause for making the apertures of the glasses small, except that the rays coming from a single point are not collected accurately at another single point, but in a small area which we generally call the mechanical point, and that this small area is greater or less in proportion to the size of the aperture. Further, I ask whether the lenses which you call "pandochæ" correct this fault, so that the mechanical point or small area, on which the rays coming from a single point are after refraction collected, always preserves the same proportional size, whether the aperture be small or large. If so, one may enlarge the aperture as much as one likes, and consequently these lenses will be far superior to those of any other shape known to me; if not, I hardly see why you praise them so greatly beyond common lenses. For circular lenses have everywhere the same axis; therefore, when we employ them, we must regard all the points of an object as placed in the optic axis; although all the points of the object be not at the same distance, the difference arising thence will not be perceptible, when the objects are very remote; because then the rays coming from a single point would, as they enter the glass, be regarded as parallel. I think your lenses might be of service in obtaining a more distinct representation of all the objects, when we wish to include several objects in one view, as we do, when we employ very large convex circular lenses. However, I would rather suspend my judgment about all these details, till you have more clearly explained your meaning, as I heartily beg you to do. I have, as you requested, sent the other copy of your paper to Mr. . . . He answers, that he has at present no time to study it, but he hopes to have leisure in a week or two.

I have not yet seen the "Prodromo" of Francis Lana, nor the "Physico-Mechanical Reflections" of John Oltius. What I more regret is, that your "Physical Hypothesis" has not yet come to my hands, nor is there a copy for sale here at the Hague. The gift, therefore, which you so liberally promised me will be most acceptable to me; if I can be of use to you in any other matter, you will always find me most ready. I hope you will not think it too irksome to reply to this short note.

Distinguished Sir,

Yours sincerely,

B. DE SPINOZA.

THE HAGUE, 9 NOV., 1671.

P.S. Mr. Diemerbroech does not live here. I am,

therefore, forced to intrust this to an ordinary letter carrier. I doubt not that you know someone at the Hague, who would take charge of our letters; I should like to hear of such a person, that our correspondence might be more conveniently and securely taken care of. If the "Tractatus Theologico-Politicus" has not yet come to your hands, I will, unless you have any objection, send you a copy. Farewell.

SPINOZA TO FABRITIUS.

[Spinoza thanks the Elector for his kind offer, but, owing to his unwillingness to teach in public, and other causes, humbly begs to be allowed time to consider it.]

DISTINGUISHED SIR,—If I had ever desired to take a professorship in any faculty, I could not have wished for any other than that which is offered to me, through you, by His Most Serene Highness the Elector Palatine, especially because of that freedom in philosophical teaching, which the most gracious prince is kind enough to grant, not to speak of the desire which I have long entertained, to live under the rule of a prince, whom all men admire for his wisdom.

But since it has never been my wish to teach in public, I have been unable to induce myself to accept this splendid opportunity, though I have long deliberated about it. I think in the first place, that I should abandon philosophical research if I consented to find time for teaching young students. I think, in the second place, that I do not know the limits, within which the freedom of my philosophical teaching would be confined, if I am to avoid all appearance of disturbing the publicly established religion. Religious quarrels do not arise so much from ardent zeal for religion, as from men's various dispositions and love of contradiction, which causes them to habitually distort and condemn everything, however rightly it may have been said. I have experienced these results in my private and secluded station, how much more should I have to fear them after my elevation to this post of honor.

Thus you see, distinguished Sir, that I am not holding back in the hope of getting something better, but through my love of quietness, which I think I can in some measure secure, if I keep away from lecturing in public. I therefore most earnestly entreat you to beg of the Most Serene Elector, that I may be allowed to consider further about this matter, and I also ask you to conciliate the favor of the most gracious prince to his most devoted admirer, thus increasing the obligations of your sincere friend,   B. DE S.

THE HAGUE, 30 March, 1673.

SPINOZA TO HUGO BOXEL.

[Spinoza answers that he does not know what ghosts are, and can gain no information from antiquity. (The Hague, Sept., 1674.)]

DEAR SIR,— Your letter, which I received yesterday, was most welcome to me, both because I wanted to hear news of you, and also because it shows that you have not utterly forgotten me. Although some might think it a bad omen, that ghosts are the cause of your writing to me, I, on the contrary, can discern a deeper meaning in the circumstance; I see that not only truths, but also things trifling and imaginary may be of use to me.

However, let us defer the question, whether ghosts are delusions and imaginary, for I see that not only denial of them, but even doubt about them seems very singular to you, as to one who has been convinced by the numerous histories related by men of to-day and the ancients. The great esteem and honor, in which I have always held and still hold you, does not suffer me to contradict you, still less to humor you. The middle course, which I shall adopt, is to beg you to be kind enough to select from the numerous stories which you have read, one or two of those least open to doubt, and most clearly demonstrating the existence of ghosts. For to confess the truth, I have never read a trustworthy author, who clearly showed that there are such things. Up to the present time I do not know what they are, and no one has ever been able to tell me. Yet it is evident, that in the case of a thing so clearly shown by experience we ought to know what it is; otherwise we shall have great difficulty in gathering from histories that ghosts exist. We only gather that something exists of nature unknown. If philosophers choose to call things which we do not know "ghosts," I shall not deny the existence of such, for there are an infinity of things, which I cannot make out.

Pray tell me, my dear Sir, before I explain myself further in the matter, What are these ghosts or spectres? Are they children, or fools, or madmen? For all that I have heard of them seems more adapted to the silly than the wise, or, to say the best we can of it, resembles the pastimes of children or of fools. Before I end, I would submit to you one consideration, namely, that the desire which most men have to narrate things, not as they really happened, but as they wished them to happen, can be illustrated from the stories of ghosts and spectres more easily than from any others. The principal reason for this is, I believe, that such stories are only attested by the narrators, and thus a fabricator can add or suppress circumstances, as seems most convenient to him, without fear of anyone being able to contradict him. He composes them to suit special circumstances, in order to justify the fear he feels of dreams and phantoms, or else to confirm his courage, his credit, or his opinion. There are other reasons, which lead me to doubt, if not the actual stories, at least some of the narrated circumstances; and which have a close bearing on the conclusion we are endeavoring to derive from the aforesaid stories. I will here stop, until I have learned from you what those stories are, which have so completely convinced you, that you regard all doubt about them as absurd, etc.

SPINOZA TO HUGO BOXEL.

[Spinoza treats of the necessary creation of the world—he refutes his friend's arguments and quotations.]

DEAR SIR,—I will rely on what you said in your letter

of the 21st of last month, that friends may disagree on indifferent questions, without injury to their friendship, and will frankly tell you my opinion on the reasons and stories, whereon you base your conclusion, that THERE ARE GHOSTS OF EVERY KIND, BUT PERHAPS NONE OF THE FEMALE SEX. The reason for my not replying sooner is that the books you quoted are not at hand, in fact I have not found any except Pliny and Suetonius. However, these two have saved me the trouble of consulting any other, for I am persuaded that they all talk in the same strain and hanker after extraordinary tales, which rouse men's astonishment and compel their wonder. I confess that I am not a little amazed, not at the stories, but at those who narrate them. I wonder that men of talent and judgment should so employ their readiness of speech, and abuse it in endeavoring to convince us of such trifles.

However, let us dismiss the writers, and turn to the question itself. In the first place, we will reason a little about your conclusion. Let us see whether I, who deny that there are spectres or spirits, am on that account less able to understand the authors, who have written on the subject; or whether you, who assert that such beings exist, do not give to the aforesaid writers more credit than they deserve. The distinction you drew, in admitting without hesitation spirits of the male sex, but doubting whether any female spirits exist, seems to me more like a fancy than a genuine doubt. If it were really your opinion, it would resemble the common imagination that God is masculine, not feminine. I wonder that those, who have seen naked ghosts, have not cast their eyes on those parts of the person, which would remove all doubt; perhaps they were timid, or did not know of this distinction. You would say that this is ridicule, not reasoning: and hence I see, that your reasons appear to you so strong and well-founded, that no one can (at least in your judgment) contradict them, unless he be some perverse fellow, who thinks the world has been made by chance. This impels me, before going into your reasons, to set forth briefly my opinion on the question, WHETHER THE WORLD WAS MADE BY CHANCE. But I answer, that as it is clear that chance and necessity are two contraries, so it is also clear, that he, who asserts the world to be a necessary effect of the divine nature, must utterly deny that the world has been made by chance; whereas, he who affirms, that God need not have made the world, confirms, though in different language, the doctrine that it has been made by chance; inasmuch as he maintains that it proceeds from a wish, which might never have been formed. However, as this opinion and theory is on the face of it absurd, it is commonly very unanimously admitted, that God's will is eternal, and has never been in-different; hence it must necessarily be also admitted, you will observe, that the world is a necessary effect of the divine nature. Let them call it will, understanding, or any name they like, they come at last to the same con-clusion, that under different names they are expressing one and the same thing. If you ask them, whether the divine will does not differ from the human, they answer, that the former has nothing in common with the latter except its name; especially as they generally admit that God's will, understanding, intellect, essence, and nature are all identical; so I, myself, lest I should confound the divine nature with the human, do not assign to God human attributes, such as will, understanding, attention, hearing, etc. I therefore say, as I have said already, that THE WORLD IS A NECESSARY EFFECT OF THE DIVINE NATURE, AND THAT IT HAS NOT BEEN MADE BY CHANCE. I think this is enough to persuade you, that the opinion of those (if such there be), who say that the world has been made by chance, is entirely contrary to mine; and, relying on this hypothesis, I proceed to examine those reasons which lead you to infer the existence of all kinds of ghosts. I should like to say of these reasons gener-ally, that they seem rather conjectures than reasons, and I can with difficulty believe, that you take them for guiding reasons. However, be they conjectures or be they reasons, let us see whether we can take them for foundations.

Your first reason is, that the existence of ghosts is needful for the beauty and perfection of the universe.

Beauty, my dear sir, is not so much a quality of the object beheld, as an effect in him who beholds it. If our sight were longer or shorter, or if our constitution were different, what now appears beautiful to us would seem misshapen, and what we now think misshapen we should regard as beautiful. The most beautiful hand seen through the microscope will appear horrible. Some things are beautiful at a distance, but ugly near; thus things regarded in themselves, and in relation to God, are neither ugly nor beautiful. Therefore, he who says that God has created the world, so that it might be beautiful, is bound to adopt one of the two alternatives, either that God created the world for the sake of men's pleasure and eyesight, or else that he created men's pleasure and eyesight for the sake of the world. Now, whether we adopt the former or the latter of these views, how God could have furthered his object by the creation of ghosts, I cannot see. Perfection and imperfection are names, which do not differ much from the names beauty and ugliness. I only ask, therefore (not to be tedious), which would contribute most to the perfect adornment of the world, ghosts, or a quantity of monsters, such as centaurs, hydras, harpies, satyrs, gryphons, arguses, and other similar inventions? Truly the world would be handsomely bedecked, if God had adorned and embellished it, in obedience to our fancy, with beings, which any one may readily imagine and dream of, but no one can understand.

Your second reason is, that because spirits express God's image more than embodied creatures, it is probable that he has created them. I frankly confess, that I am as yet in ignorance, how spirits more than other creatures express God. This I know, that between finite and infinite there is no comparison; so that the difference between God and the greatest and most excellent created thing is no less than the difference between God and the least created thing. This argument, therefore, is beside the mark. If I had as clear an idea of ghosts as I have of a triangle or a circle, I should not in the least hesitate to affirm that they had been created by

God; but as the idea I possess of them is just like the ideas, which my imagination forms of harpies, gryphons, hydras, etc., I cannot consider them as anything but dreams, which differ from God as totally, as that which is not differs from that which is.

Your third reason (that as body exists without soul, so soul should exist without body) seems to me equally absurd. Pray tell me, if it is not also likely, that memory, hearing, sight, etc., exist without bodies, because bodies exist without memory, hearing, sight, etc., or that a sphere exists without a circle, because a circle exists without a sphere ?

Your fourth, and last reason, is the same as your first, and I refer you to my answer given above. I will only observe here, that I do not know which are the highest or which the lowest places, which you conceive as existing in infinite matter, unless you take the earth as the centre of the universe. For if the sun or Saturn be the centre of the universe, the sun or Saturn, not the earth, will be the lowest.

Thus, passing by this argument and what remains, I conclude, that these and similar reasons will convince no one of the existence of all kinds of ghosts and spectres, unless it be those persons, who shut their ears to the understanding, and allow themselves to be led away by superstition. This last is so hostile to right reason, that she lends willing credence to old wives' tales for the sake of discrediting philosophers.

As regards the stories, I have already said in my first letter, that I do not deny them altogether, but only the conclusion drawn from them. To this I may add, that I do not believe them so thoroughly, as not to doubt many of the details, which are generally added rather for ornament than for bringing out the truth of the story or the conclusion drawn from it. I had hoped, that out of so many stories you would at least have produced one or two, which could hardly be questioned, and which would clearly show that ghosts or spectres exist. The case you relate of the burgomaster, who wanted to infer their existence, because he heard spectral brewers working in his mother's brew-house by night, and making the same noises as he was accustomed to hear by day, seems to me laughable. In like manner it would be tedious here to examine all the stories of people, who have written on these trifles. To be brief, I cite the instance of Julius Cæsar, who, as Suetonius testifies, laughed at such things and yet was happy, if we may trust what Suetonius says in the 59th chapter of his life of that leader. And so should all, who reflect on the human imagination, and the effects of the emotions, laugh at such notions; whatever Lavater and others, who have gone dreaming with him in the matter, may produce to the contrary.

SPINOZA TO HUGO BOXEL.

[Spinoza again answers the argument in favor of ghosts. (The Hague, 1674.)]

DEAR SIR,— I hasten to answer your letter, received yesterday, for if I delay my reply, I may have to put it off longer than I should like. The state of your health would have made me anxious, if I did not understand that you are better. I hope you are by this time quite well again.

The difficulties experienced by two people following different principles, and trying to agree on a matter, which depends on many other questions, might be shown from this discussion alone, if there were no reason to prove it by. Pray tell me, whether you have seen or read any philosophers, who hold that the world has been made by chance, taking chance in your sense, namely, that God had some design in making the world and yet has not kept to the plan he had formed. I do not know, that such an idea has ever entered anyone's mind. I am likewise at a loss for the reasons, with which you want to make me believe, that chance and necessity are not contraries. As soon as I affirm that the three angles of a triangle are equal to two right angles necessarily, I deny that they are thus equal by chance. As soon as I affirm that heat is a necessary effect of fire, I deny that it is a chance effect. To say that necessary and free are two contrary terms, seems to me no less absurd and repugnant to reason. For no one can deny, that God freely knows himself and all else, yet all with one voice grant that God knows himself necessarily. Hence as it seems to me, you draw no distinction between constraint or force and necessity. Man's wishes to live, to love, etc., are not under constraint, but nevertheless are necessary; much more is it necessary that God wishes to be, to know, and to act. If you will also reflect, that indifference is only another name for ignorance or doubt, and that a will always constant and determined in all things is a necessary property of the understanding, you will see that my words are in complete harmony with truth. If we affirm, that God might have been able not to wish a given event, or not to understand it, we attribute to God two different freedoms, one necessary, the other indifferent; consequently we shall conceive God's will as different from his essence and understanding, and shall thus fall from one absurdity into another.

The attention, which I asked for in my former letter, has not seemed to you necessary. This has been the reason why you have not directed your thoughts to the main issue, and have neglected a point which is very important.

Further, when you say that if I deny, that the operations of seeing, hearing, attending, wishing, etc., can be ascribed to God, or that they exist in him in any eminent fashion, you do not know what sort of God mine is: I suspect that you believe there is no greater perfection than such as can be explained by the aforesaid attributes. I am not astonished; for I believe that, if a triangle could speak, it would say, in like manner, that God is eminently triangular, while a circle would say that the divine nature is eminently circular. Thus each would ascribe to God its own attributes, would assume itself to be like God, and look on everything else as ill-shaped.

The briefness of a letter and want of time do not allow me to enter into my opinion on the divine nature, or the questions you have propounded. Besides, suggesting difficulties is not the same as producing reasons. That we do many things in the world from conjecture is true, but that our reflections are based on conjectures is false. In practical life we are compelled to follow what is most probable; in speculative thought we are compelled to follow truth. A man would perish of hunger and thirst, if he refused to eat or drink, till he had obtained positive proof that food and drink would be good for him. But in philosophic reflection this is not so. On the contrary, we must take care not to admit as true anything, which is only probable. For when one falsity has been let in, infinite others follow.

Again, we cannot infer that because sciences of things divine and human are full of controversies and quarrels, therefore their whole subject-matter is uncertain; for there have been many persons so enamored of contradiction, as to turn into ridicule geometrical axioms. Sextus Empiricus and other sceptics, whom you quote, declare, that it is false to say that a whole is greater than its part, and pass similar judgments on other axioms.

However, as I pass over and grant that in default of proof we must be content with probabilities, I say that a probable proof ought to be such that, though we may doubt about it, we cannot maintain its contrary; for that which can be contradicted resembles not truth but falsehood. For instance, if I say that Peter is alive, because I saw him yesterday in good health, this is a prob︎︎︎ility, in so far as no one can maintain the contrary; but if anyone says that he saw Peter yesterday in a swoon, and that he believed Peter to have departed this life to-day, he will make my statement seem false. That conjecture about ghosts and spectres seems false, and not even probable, I have shown so clearly, that I can find nothing worthy of answer in your reply.

To your question, whether I have of God as clear an idea as I have of a triangle, I reply in the affirmative. But if you ask me, whether I have as clear a mental image of God as I have of a triangle, I reply in the negative. For we are not able to imagine God, though we can understand him. You must also here observe, that I do not assert that I thoroughly know God, but that I understand some of his attributes, not all nor the greater part, and it is evident that my ignorance of very many does not hinder the knowledge I have of some. When I learned Euclid's Elements, I understood that the three angles of a triangle are equal to two right angles, and this property of a triangle I perceived clearly, though I might be ignorant of many others.

As regards spectres or ghosts, I have hitherto heard attributed to them no intelligible property: they seem like phantoms, which no one can understand. When you say that spectres, or ghosts, in these lower regions (I adopt your phraseology, though I know not why matter below should be inferior to matter above) consist in a very thin rarefied and subtle substance, you seem to me to be speaking of spiders' webs, air, or vapors. To say, that they are invisible, seems to me to be equivalent to saying that they do not exist, not to stating their nature; unless, perhaps, you wish to indicate, that they render themselves visible or invisible at will, and that the imagination, in these as in other impossibilities, will find a difficulty.

The authority of Plato, Aristotle, and Socrates, does not carry much weight with me. I should have been astonished, if you had brought forward Epicurus, Democritus, Lucretius, or any of the atomists, or upholders of the atomic theory. It is no wonder that persons, who have invented occult qualities, intentional species, substantial forms, and a thousand other trifles, should have also devised spectres and ghosts, and given credence to old wives' tales, in order to take away the reputation of Democritus, whom they were so jealous of, that they burned all the books which he had published amid so much eulogy. If you are inclined to believe such witnesses, what reason have you for denying the miracles of the Blessed Virgin, and all the Saints? These have been described by so many famous philosophers, theologians, and historians, that I could produce at least a hundred such authorities for every one of the former.

cerptam & defcriptam effe neceffariò fatendum eſt, adeo parum
ſibi conſtare videmus. Cap. enim 47. Geneſ. narrat quod Jahacob
cum primum Pharahonem ducente Joſepho ſalutavit, annos 130.
natus erat, à quibus ſi auferantur viginti duo, quos propter Joſephi
abſentiam in mœrore tranſegit & præterea ſeptemdecim ætatis Joſephi cum venderetur, & denique ſeptem, quos propter Rachelem
ſervivit, reperietur ipſum provectiſſimæ ætatis fuiſſe, octoginta ſci-
licet & quatuor annorum cum Leam in uxorem duceret, & contra
Dinam vix ſeptem fuiſſe annorum; cum à Sechemo vim paſſa eſt,
Simeon autem & Levi vix duodecim & undecim, cum totam illam
civitatem deprædati ſunt, ejuſque omnes cives gladio confecerunt.
Nec hic opus habeo omnia Pentateuchi recenſere, ſi quis modo ad
hoc attenderit, quod in hiſce quinque libris omnia præcepta ſcili-
cet & hiſtoriæ promiſcue ſine ordinē narrentur, neque ratio tem-
porum habeatur, & quod una eademque hiſtoria ſæpe, & aliquan-
do diverſimode repetatur, facile dignoſcet hæc omnia promiſcue
collecta, & coacervata fuiſſe, ut poſtea facilius examinarentur, &
in ordinem redigerentur. At non tantum hæc quæ in quinque libris, ſed etiam reliquæ hiſtoriæ uſque ad vaſtationem urbis, quæ
in reliquis ſeptem libris continentur, eodem modo collectæ ſunt.
Quis enim non videt, in cap. 2. Judicum ex verſ. 6. novum hiſtori-
cum adſerri (qui res à Joſua geſtas etiam ſcripſerat) ejuſque verba
ſimpliciter deſcribi. Nam poſtquam hiſtoricus noſter in ult. cap.
Joſuæ narravit, quod ipſe mortem obierit, quædque ſepultus fue-
rit & in primo hujus libri narrare ea promiſerit quæ poſt ejuſdem
mortem contigerunt, qua ratione, ſi filum ſuæ hiſtoriæ ſequi vole-
bat, potuiſſet ſuperioribus annectere, quæ hîc de ipſo Joſua narrare incipit. Sic etiam capita 17. 18. &c. Samuëlis 1. ex alio hiſto-
rico deſumta ſunt, qui aliam cauſam ſentiebat fuiſſe, cur David
aulam Saulis frequentare inceperit, longe diverſam ab illa, quæ in
cap. 16. libri ejuſdem narratur: non enim ſenſit quod David ex
conſilio ſervorum à Saulo vocatus ipſum adiit (ut in cap. 16. narratur) ſed quod caſu à patre ad fratres in caſtra miſſus Saulo ex occa-
ſione victoriæ, quam contra Philiſtæum Goliat habuit, tum demum
innotuit, & in aula detentus fuit. Idem de cap. 26. ejuſdem libri
P 3   ſuſpi-

[marginal handwritten notes in Latin, in Spinoza's hand]

[lower margin: handwritten notes in Latin, in Spinoza's hand]

Marginal Notes to Spinoza's *Tractatus Theologico-Politicus*
(1670) in his own handwriting.

But I have gone further, my dear Sir, than I intended: I do not desire to cause any further annoyance by doctrines which I know you will not grant. For the principles which you follow are far different from my own.

SPINOZA TO SCHULLER (THE HAGUE, OCTOBER 1674.)

[Spinoza gives his opinions on liberty and necessity.]

SIR:—Our friend, J. R., has sent me the letter which you have been kind enough to write to me, and also the judgment of your friend as to the opinions of Descartes and myself regarding free will. Both inclosures were very welcome to me. Though I am, at present, much occupied with other matters, not to mention my delicate health, your singular courtesy, or, to name the chief motive, your love of truth, impels me to satisfy your inquiries, as far as my poor abilities will permit. What your friend wishes to imply by his remark before he appeals to experience, I know not. What he adds, that WHEN ONE OF TWO DISPUTANTS AFFIRMS SOMETHING WHICH THE OTHER DENIES, BOTH MAY BE RIGHT, is true, if he means that the two, though using the same terms, are thinking of different things. I once sent several examples of this to our friend J. R., and am now writing to tell him to communicate them to you.

I, therefore, pass on to that definition of liberty, which he says is my own; but I know not whence he has taken it. I say that a thing is free, which exists and acts solely by the necessity of its own nature. Thus also God understands himself and all things freely, because it follows solely from the necessity of his nature, that he should understand all things. You see I do not place freedom in free decision, but in free necessity. However, let us descend to created things, which are all determined by external causes to exist and operate in a given determinate manner. In order that this may be clearly understood, let us conceive a very simple thing. For instance, a stone receives from the impulsion of an external cause, a certain quantity of motion, by virtue of which it continues to move after the impulsion given by the external cause has ceased. The permanence of the stone's motion is constrained, not necessarily, because it must be defined by the impulsion of an external cause. What is true of the stone is true of any individual, however complicated its nature, or varied its functions, inasmuch as every individual thing is necessarily determined by some external cause to exist and operate in a fixed and determinate manner.

Further conceive, I beg, that a stone, while continuing in motion, should be capable of thinking and knowing, that it is endeavoring, as far as it can, to continue to move. Such a stone, being conscious merely of its own endeavor and not at all indifferent, would believe itself to be completely free, and would think that it continued in motion solely because of its own wish. This is that human freedom, which all boast that they possess, and which consists solely in the fact, that men are conscious of their own desire, but are ignorant of the causes whereby that desire has been determined. Thus an infant believes that it desires milk freely; an angry child thinks he wishes freely for vengeance, a timid child thinks he wishes freely to run away. Again, a drunken man thinks, that from the free decision of his mind he speaks words, which afterward, when sober, he would like to have left unsaid. So the delirious, the garrulous, and others of the same sort think that they act from the free decision of their mind, not that they are carried away by impulse. As this misconception is innate in all men, it is not easily conquered. For, although experience abundantly shows, that men can do anything rather than check their desires, and that very often, when a prey to conflicting emotions, they see the better course and follow the worse, they yet believe themselves to be free; because in some cases their desire for a thing is slight, and can easily be overruled by the recollection of something else, which is frequently present in the mind.

I have thus, if I mistake not, sufficiently explained my

opinion regarding free and constrained necessity, and also regarding so-called human freedom: from what I have said you will easily be able to reply to your friend's objections. For when he says, with Descartes, that he who is constrained by no external cause is free, if by being constrained he means acting against one's will, I grant that we are in some cases quite unrestrained, and in this respect possess free will. But if by constrained he means acting necessarily, although not against one's will (as I have explained above), I deny that we are in any instance free.

But your friend, on the contrary, asserts that WE MAY EMPLOY OUR REASON ABSOLUTELY, THAT IS, IN COMPLETE FREEDOM; and is, I think, a little too confident on the point. FOR WHO, he says, COULD DENY, WITHOUT CONTRADICTING HIS OWN CONSCIOUSNESS, THAT I CAN THINK WITH MY THOUGHTS, THAT I WISH OR DO NOT WISH TO WRITE? I should like to know what consciousness he is talking of, over and above that which I have illustrated by the example of the stone.

As a matter of fact I, without, I hope, contradicting my consciousness, that is my reason and experience, and without cherishing ignorance and misconception, deny that I can by any absolute power of thought think, that I wish or do not wish to write. I appeal to the consciousness, which he has doubtless experienced, that in dreams he has not the power of thinking that he wishes, or does not wish to write; and that, when he dreams that he wishes to write, he has not the power not to dream that he wishes to write. I think he must also have experienced, that the mind is not always equally capable of thinking of the same object, but according as the body is more capable for the image of this or that object being excited in it, so is the mind more capable of thinking of the same object.

When he further adds, that the causes for his applying his mind to writing have led him, but not constrained him to write, he merely means (if he will look at the question impartially), that his disposition was then in a state, in which it could easily be acted on by causes, which would have been powerless under other circumstances, as for instance, when he was under a violent emotion. That is, causes, which at other times would not have constrained him, have constrained him, in this case, not to write against his will, but necessarily to wish to write.

As for his statement, that IF WE WERE CONSTRAINED BY EXTERNAL CAUSES, NO ONE COULD ACQUIRE THE HABIT OF VIRTUE, I know not what is his authority for saying, that firmness and constancy of disposition cannot arise from predestined necessity, but only from free will.

What he finally adds, that IF THIS WERE GRANTED, ALL WICKEDNESS WOULD BE EXCUSABLE, I meet with the question, What then? Wicked men are not less to be feared, and are not less harmful, when they are wicked from necessity. However, on this point I would ask you to refer to my "Principles of Cartesian Philosophy," Part II., chap. viii.

In a word, I should like your friend, who makes these objections, to tell me, how he reconciles the human virtue, which he says arises from the free decision of the mind, with God's pre-ordainment of the universe. If, with Descartes, he confesses his inability to do so, he is endeavoring to direct against me the weapon which has already pierced himself. But in vain. For if you examine my opinion attentively, you will see that it is quite consistent, etc.

SPINOZA TO TSCHIRNHAUS

[The difference between a true and an adequate idea is merely extrinsic, etc. The Hague, Jan., 1675.]

HONORED SIR.—Between a true and an adequate idea, I recognize no difference, except that the epithet true only has regard to the agreement between the idea and its object, whereas the epithet adequate has regard to the nature of the idea in itself; so that in reality there is no difference between a true and an adequate idea beyond this extrinsic relation. However, in order that I may know, from which idea out of many all the properties of its object may be deduced, I pay attention to one point only, namely, that the idea or definition should express the efficient cause of its object. For instance, in inquiring into the properties of a circle, I ask, whether from the idea of a circle, that it consists of infinite right angles, I can deduce all its properties. I ask, I repeat, whether this idea involves the efficient cause of a circle. If it does not, I look for another, namely, that a circle is the space described by a line, of which one point is fixed, and the other movable. As this definition explains the efficient cause, I know that I can deduce from it all the properties of a circle. So, also, when I define God as a supremely perfect Being, then, since that definition does not express the efficient cause (I mean the efficient cause internal as well as external) I shall not be able to infer therefrom all the properties of God; as I can, when I define God as a Being, etc. (see "Ethics," I. Def. vi.). As for your other inquiries, namely, that concerning motion, and those pertaining to method, my observations on them are not yet written out in due order, so I will reserve them for another occasion.

As regards your remark, that he "who considers lines applied to curves makes many deductions with regard to the measurement of curves, but does so with greater facility from the consideration of tangents," etc., I think that from the consideration of tangents many deductions will be made with more difficulty, than from the consideration of lines applied in succession; and I assert absolutely, that from certain properties of any particular thing (whatever idea be given) some things may be discovered more readily, others with more difficulty, though all are concerned with the nature of the thing. I think it need only be observed, that an idea should be sought for of such a kind, that all properties may be inferred, as has been said above. He who is about to deduce all the properties of a particular thing, knows that the ultimate properties will necessarily be the most difficult to discover, etc.

DEAR SIR,—I am glad that you have at last had occasion to refresh me with one of your letters, always most welcome to me. I heartily beg that you will frequently repeat the favor, etc.

I proceed to consider your doubts: to the first I answer, that the human mind can only acquire knowledge of those things which the idea of a body actually existing involves, or of what can be inferred from such an idea. For the power of anything is defined solely by its essence ("Ethics," III. vii.); the essence of the mind ("Ethics," II. xiii.) consists solely in this, that it is the idea of body actually existing; therefore, the mind's power of understanding only extends to things, which this idea of body contains in itself, or which follow therefrom. Now this idea of body does not involve or express any of God's attributes, save extension and thought. For its object (*ideatum*), namely, body (by "Ethics," II. vi.) has God for its cause, in so far as he is regarded under the attribute of extension, and not in so far as he is regarded under any other; therefore ("Ethics," I. Ax. vi.), this idea of the body involves the knowledge of God, only in so far as he is regarded under the attribute of extension. Further, this idea, in so far as it is a mode of thinking, has also (by the same proposition) God for its cause, in so far as he is regarded as a thinking thing, and not in so far as he is regarded under any other attribute. Hence (by the same axiom) the idea of this idea involves the knowledge of God, in so far as he is regarded under the attribute of thought, and not in so far as he is regarded under any attribute. It is therefore plain, that the human mind, or the idea of the human body neither involves nor expresses any attributes to God save these two. Now from these two attributes, or their modifications, no other attribute of God can ("Ethics," I. x.) be inferred or conceived. I therefore conclude that the human mind cannot attain knowledge of any attribute of God besides these, which is the proposition you inquire about. With regard to your question, whether there must be as many worlds as there are attributes, I refer you to "Ethics," II. vii. note.

Moreover, this proposition might be proved more readily by a reduction to the absurd; I am accustomed, when the proposition is negative, to employ this mode of demonstration as more in character. However, as the question you ask is positive, I make use of the positive method, and ask, whether one thing can be produced from another, from which it differs both in essence and existence; for things which differ to this extent seem to have nothing in common. But since all particular things, except those which are produced from things similar to themselves, differ from their causes both in essence and existence, I see here no reason for doubt.

The sense in which I mean that God is the efficient cause of things, no less of their essence than of their existence, I think has been sufficiently explained in "Ethics" I. xxv. note and corollary. The axiom in the note to "Ethics" I. x., as I hinted at the end of the said note, is based on the idea which we have of a Being absolutely infinite, not on the fact, that there are or may be beings possessing three, four or more attributes.

Lastly, the examples you ask for of the first kind are, in thought, absolutely infinite understanding; in extension, motion and rest; an example of the second kind is the sum of the whole extended universe (*facies totius universi*), which, though it varies in infinite modes, yet remains always the same. *Cf.* "Ethics" II. note to Lemma vii. before Prop. xiv.

Thus, most excellent Sir, I have answered, as I think, the objections of yourself and your friend. If you think any uncertainty remains, I hope you will not neglect to tell me, so that I may, if possible, remove it.

THE HAGUE, 29 July, 1675.

[In this fragment of a letter Spinoza refers his friend to "Ethics,"
I. x. and II. vii. note.]

DISTINGUISHED SIR,— . . . But in answer to your
objection I say, that although each particular thing be
expressed in infinite ways in the infinite understanding
of God, yet those infinite ideas, whereby it is expressed,
cannot constitute one and the same mind of a particular
thing, but infinite minds; seeing that each of these infinite ideas has no connection with the rest, as I have
explained in the same note to " Ethics," II. vii., and as is
also evident from I. x. If you will reflect on these
passages a little, you will see that all difficulty vanishes,
etc.

THE HAGUE, 18 August, 1675.

SPINOZA TO SCHULLER

[Spinoza answers all the points in Schuller's letter, and hesitates to
intrust his writings to Leibniuz.]

MOST EXPERIENCED SIR, AND VALUED FRIEND,— I was
much pleased to learn from your letter, received to-day,
that you are well, and that our friend von Tschirnhausen
has happily accomplished his journey to France. In the
conversation which he had about me with Mr. Huygens,
he behaved, at least in my opinion, very judiciously; and
besides, I am very glad that he has found so convenient
an opportunity for the purpose which he intended. But
what it is he has found in the fourth axiom of Part I.
that seems to contradict Proposition v. of Part II. I do
not see. For in that proposition it is affirmed, that the
essence of every idea has for its cause God, in so far as
he is considered as a thinking thing; but in that axiom,
that the knowledge or idea of a cause depends on the
knowledge or idea of an effect. But, to tell the truth,

I do not quite follow, in this matter, the meaning of your letter, and suspect that either in it, or in his copy of the book, there is a slip of the pen. For you write, that it is affirmed in Proposition v. that the objects of ideas are the efficient causes of the ideas, whereas this is exactly what is expressly denied in that proposition, and I now think that this is the cause of the whole confusion. Accordingly it would be useless for me at present to try to write at greater length on this subject, but I must wait till you explain to me his mind more clearly, and till I know whether he has a correct copy. I believe that I have an epistolary acquaintance with the Leibnitz he mentions. But why he, who was a counselor at Frankfort, has gone to France, I do not know. As far as I could conjecture from his letters, he seemed to me a man of liberal mind, and versed in every science. But yet I think it imprudent so soon to intrust my writings to him. I should like first to know what is his business in France, and the judgment of our friend von Tschirnhausen, when he has been longer in his company, and knows his character more intimately. However, greet that friend of ours in my name, and let him command me what he pleases, if in anything I can be of service to him, and he will find me most ready to obey him in everything.

I congratulate my most worthy friend Mr. Bresser on his arrival or return, and also thank him heartily for the promised beer, and will requite him, too, in anyway that I can. Lastly, I have not yet tried to find out your relation's method, nor do I think that I shall be able to apply my mind to trying it. For the more I think over the thing in itself, the more I am persuaded that you have not made gold, but had not sufficiently eliminated that which was hidden in the antimony. But more of this another time: at present I am prevented by want of leisure. In the meanwhile, if in anything I can assist you, you will always find me, most excellent sir, your friend and devoted servant,

B. DE SPINOZA.

THE HAGUE, 18 NOV., 1675.

[Spinoza explains his view of the infinite.]

DISTINGUISHED SIR,— My statement concerning the infinite, that an infinity of parts cannot be inferred from a multitude of parts, is plain when we consider that if such a conclusion could be drawn from a multitude of parts, we should not be able to imagine a greater multitude of parts; the first-named multitude, whatever it was, would have to be the greater, which is contrary to fact. For in the whole space between two non-concentric circles we conceive a greater multitude of parts than in half that space, yet the number of parts in the half, as in the whole of the space, exceeds any assignable number. Again, from extension, as Descartes conceives it, to wit, a quiescent mass, it is not only difficult, as you say, but absolutely impossible, to prove the existence of bodies. For matter at rest, as it is in itself, will continue at rest, and will only be determined to motion by some more powerful external cause; for this reason I have not hesitated on a former occasion to affirm, that the Cartesian principles of natural things are useless, not to say absurd.

THE HAGUE, 5 May, 1676.

SPINOZA TO TSCHIRNHAUS

[Spinoza gives the required explanation. Mentions the treatise of Huet, etc.]

DISTINGUISHED SIR,— With regard to your question as to whether the variety of the universe can be deduced *a priori* from the conception of extension only, I believe I have shown clearly enough already that it cannot; and that, therefore, matter has been ill-defined by Descartes as extension; it must necessarily be explained through an attribute, which expresses eternal and infinite essence. But perhaps, some day, if my life be prolonged, I may discuss the subject with you more clearly. For hitherto

I have not been able to put any of these matters into due order.

As to what you add; namely, that from the definition of a given thing considered in itself we can only deduce a single property, this is, perhaps, true in the case of very simple things (among which I count figures), but not in realities. For, from the fact alone, that I define God as a being to whose essence belongs existence, I infer several of his properties; namely, that he necessarily exists, that he is one, unchangeable, infinite, etc. I could adduce several other examples, which, for the present, I pass over.

In conclusion, I ask you to inquire, whether Huet's treatise (against the "Tractatus Theologico-Politicus"), about which I wrote to you before, has yet been published, and whether you could send me a copy. Also, whether you yet know, what are the new discoveries about refraction. And so farewell, dear sir, and continue to regard yours, etc.

THE HAGUE, 15 July, 1676.

SPINOZA TO ALBERT BURGH.

[Spinoza laments the step taken by his pupil and answers his arguments. The Hague, end of 1675.]

THAT, which I could scarcely believe when told me by others, I learn at last from your own letter; not only have you been made a member of the Romish Church, but you are become a very keen champion of the same, and have already learned wantonly to insult and rail against your opponents.

At first I resolved to leave your letter unanswered, thinking that time and experience will assuredly be of more avail than reasoning, to restore you to yourself and your friends; not to mention other arguments, which won your approval formerly, when we were discussing the case of Steno,* in whose steps you are now following. But some of my friends, who, like myself had formed great hopes from your superior talents, strenuously urge me not

* A Danish anatomist, who renounced Lutheranism for Catholicism at Florence in 1669.

103

to fail in the offices of a friend, but to consider what you lately were, rather than what you are, with other arguments of the like nature. I have thus been induced to write you this short reply, which I earnestly beg you will think worthy of calm perusal.

I will not imitate those adversaries of Romanism, who would set forth the vices of priests and popes with a view to kindling your aversion. Such considerations are often put forward from evil and unworthy motives, and tend rather to irritate than to instruct. I will even admit, that more men of learning and of blameless life are found in the Romish Church than in any other Christian body; for, as it contains more members, so will every type of character be more largely represented in it. You cannot possibly deny, unless you have lost your memory as well as your reason, that in every church there are thoroughly honorable men, who worship God with justice and charity. We have known many such among the Lutherans, the Reformed Church, the Mennonites, and the Enthusiasts. Not to go further, you knew your own relations, who in the time of the Duke of Alva suffered every kind of torture bravely and willingly for the sake of their religion. In fact, you must admit, that personal holiness is not peculiar to the Romish Church, but common to all churches.

As it is by this, that we know "that we dwell in God and he in us" (1 Ep. John, iv. 13), it follows, that what distinguishes the Roman Church from others must be something entirely superfluous, and therefore founded solely on superstition. For, as John says, justice and charity are the one sure sign of the true Catholic faith, and the true fruits of the Holy Spirit. Wherever they are found, there in truth is Christ; wherever they are absent, Christ is absent also. For only by the spirit of Christ can we be led to the love of justice and charity. Had you been willing to reflect on these points, you would not have ruined yourself, nor have brought deep affliction on your relations, who are now sorrowfully bewailing your evil case.

But I return to your letter, which you begin, by lamenting that I allow myself to be ensnared by the prince of evil spirits. Pray take heart and recollect yourself. When you had the use of your faculties, you were wont, if I mistake not, to worship an infinite God, by whose efficacy all things absolutely come to pass and are preserved; now you dream of a prince, God's enemy, who against God's will ensnares and deceives very many men (rarely good ones, to be sure), whom God thereupon hands over to this master of wickedness to be tortured eternally. The Divine justice therefore allows the devil to deceive men and remain unpunished; but it by no means allows to remain unpunished the men, who have been by that self-same devil miserably deceived and ensnared.

These absurdities might so far be tolerated, if you worshipped a God infinite and eternal; not one whom Chastillon in the town which the Dutch call Tienen, gave with impunity to horses to be eaten. And, poor wretch, you bewail me? My philosophy, which you never beheld, you style a chimera? O youth, deprived of understanding, who has bewitched you into believing, that the supreme and eternal is eaten by you, and held in your intestines?

Yet you seem to wish to employ reason, and ask me, "HOW I KNOW THAT MY PHILOSOPHY IS THE BEST AMONG ALL THAT HAVE EVER BEEN TAUGHT IN THE WORLD, OR ARE BEING TAUGHT, OR EVER WILL BE TAUGHT?" a question which I might with much greater right ask you; for I do not presume that I have found the best philosophy, I know that I understand the true philosophy. If you ask in what way I know it, I answer: In the same way as you know that the three angles of a triangle are equal to two right angles: that this is sufficient, will be denied by no one whose brain is sound, and who does not go dreaming of evil spirits inspiring us with false ideas like the true. For the truth is the index of itself and of what is false.

But you, who presume that you have at last found the best religion, or rather the best men, on whom you have pinned your credulity, you, "WHO KNOW THAT THEY ARE THE BEST AMONG ALL WHO HAVE TAUGHT, DO NOW TEACH,

OR SHALL IN FUTURE TEACH OTHER RELIGIONS. HAVE YOU EXAMINED ALL RELIGIONS, ANCIENT AS WELL AS MODERN, TAUGHT HERE AND IN INDIA AND EVERYWHERE THROUGHOUT THE WORLD? And, IF YOU HAVE DULY EXAMINED THEM, HOW DO YOU KNOW THAT YOU HAVE CHOSEN THE BEST," since you can give no reason for the faith that is in you? But you will say, that you acquiesce in the inward testimony of the spirit of God, while the rest of mankind are ensnared and deceived by the prince of evil spirits. But all those outside the pale of the Romish Church can with equal right proclaim of their own creed what you proclaim of yours.

As to what you add of the common consent of myriads of men and the uninterrupted ecclesiastical succession, this is the very catch-word of the Pharisees. They with no less confidence than the devotees of Rome bring forward their myriad witnesses, who as pertinaciouly as the Roman witnesses repeat what they have heard, as though it were their personal experience. Further, they carry back their line to Adam. They boast with equal arrogance, that their Church has continued to this day unmoved and unimpaired in spite of the hatred of Christians and heathen. They more than any other sect are supported by antiquity. They exclaim with one voice, that they have received their traditions from God himself, and that they alone preserve the Word of God both written and unwritten. That all heresies have issued from them, and that they have remained constant through thousands of years under no constraint of temporal dominion, but by the sole efficacy of their superstition, no one can deny. The miracles they tell of would tire a thousand tongues. But their chief boast is, that they count a far greater number of martyrs than any other nation, a number which is daily increased by those who suffer with singular constancy for the faith they profess; nor is their boasting false. I myself knew among others of a certain Judah called the faithful,* who in the midst of the flames, when he was already

---

* "Don Lope de Vera y Alarcon de San Clemente, a Spanish nobleman who was converted to Judaism through the study of Hebrew, and was burnt at Valladolid on the 25th July, 1644."— POLLOCK's "Spinoza" chap. ii., last note.

thought to be dead, lifted his voice to sing the hymn beginning, "To Thee, O God, I offer up my soul," and so singing, perished.

The organization of the Roman Church, which you so greatly praise, I confess to be politic, and to many lucrative. I should believe that there was no other more convenient for deceiving the people and keeping men's minds in check, if it were not for the organization of the Mahometan Church, which far surpasses it. For from the time when this superstition arose, there has been no schism in its church.

If, therefore, you had rightly judged, you would have seen that only your third point tells in favor of the Christians, namely, that unlearned and common men should have been able to convert nearly the whole world to a belief in Christ. But this reason militates not only for the Romish Church, but for all those who profess the name of Christ.

But assume that all the reasons you bring forward tell in favor solely of the Romish Church. Do you think that you can thereby prove mathematically the authority of that Church? As the case is far otherwise, why do you wish me to believe that my demonstrations are inspired by the prince of evil spirits, while your own are inspired by God, especially as I see, and as your letter clearly shows, that you have been led to become a devotee of this Church not by your love of God, but by your fear of hell, the single cause of superstition? Is this your humility, that you trust nothing to yourself, but everything to others, who are condemned by many of their fellow men? Do you set it down to pride and arrogance, that I employ reason and acquiesce in this true Word of God, which is in the mind and can never be depraved or corrupted? Cast away this deadly superstition, acknowledge the reason which God has given you, and follow that, unless you would be numbered with the brutes. Cease, I say, to call ridiculous errors mysteries, and do not basely confound those things which are unknown to us, or have not yet been discovered, with what is proved to be absurd, like the horrible secrets of this Church of yours, which, in proportion as they are repugnant to right reason, you believe to transcend the understanding.

But the fundamental principle of the "Tractatus Theologico-Politicus," that Scripture should only be expounded through Scripture, which you so wantonly without any reason proclaim to be false, is not merely assumed, but categorically proved to be true or sound; especially in chapter vii., where also the opinions of adversaries are confuted; see also what is proved at the end of chapter xv. If you will reflect on these things, and also examine the history of the Church (of which I see you are completely ignorant), in order to see how false, in many respects, is Papal tradition, and by what course of events and with what cunning the Pope of Rome six hundred years after Christ obtained supremacy over the Church, I do not doubt that you will eventually return to your senses. That this result may come to pass I, for your sake, heartily wish. Farewell, etc.

Spinoza to Lambert van Velthuysen

(Doctor of Medicine at Utrecht).

[Of the proposed annotation of the "Tractatus Theologico-Politicus."]

MOST EXCELLENT AND DISTINGUISHED SIR,—I wonder at our friend Neustadt having said, that I am meditating the refutation of the various writings circulated against my book,* and that among the works for me to refute he places your MS. For I certainly have never entertained the intention of refuting any of my adversaries: they all seem to me utterly unworthy of being answered. I do not remember to have said to Mr. Neustadt anything more, than that I proposed to illustrate some of the obscurer passages in the treatise with notes, and that I should add to these your MS., and my answer, if your consent could be gained, on which last point I begged him to speak to you, adding, that if you refused permission on the ground that some of the observations in

* The "Tractatus Theologico-Politicus."

my answer were too harshly put, you should be given full power to modify or expunge them. In the meanwhile, I am by no means angry with Mr. Neustadt, but I wanted to put the matter before you as it stands, that if your permission be not granted, I might show you that I have no wish to publish your MS. against your will. Though I think it might be issued without endangering your reputation, if it appears without your name, I will take no steps in the matter, unless you give me leave. But, to tell the truth, you would do me a far greater kindness, if you would put in writing the arguments with which you think you can impugn my treatise, and add them to your MS. I most earnestly beg you to do this. For there is no one whose arguments I would more willingly consider; knowing, as I do, that you are bound solely by your zeal for truth, and that your mind is singularly candid. I therefore beg you again and again, not to shrink from undertaking this task, and to believe me,   Yours most obediently,

B. DE SPINOZA.